WALKING COUNTRY

HARROGATE and the WHARFE VALLEY

PUB WALKS

Valerie Yewdall

Illustrated by
Paul Hannon

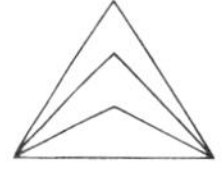

HILLSIDE

HILLSIDE GUIDES

■ *New series - Walking Country*
ILKLEY MOOR
NIDDERDALE
BOWLAND

■ *Pub Walks*
HARROGATE/WHARFE VALLEY (Valerie Yewdall)

■ *Long distance walks*
THE COAST TO COAST WALK
DALES WAY COMPANION
CLEVELAND WAY COMPANION
THE WESTMORLAND WAY
THE CUMBERLAND WAY
NORTH BOWLAND TRAVERSE (David Johnson)

■ *Large format colour hardback*
FREEDOM OF THE DALES

■ *Circular walks - Yorkshire Dales*
WALKS IN WHARFEDALE
RAMBLES IN WHARFEDALE
WALKS IN THE CRAVEN DALES
WALKS IN THREE PEAKS COUNTRY
WALKS IN WENSLEYDALE
WALKS IN SWALEDALE
WALKS ON THE HOWGILL FELLS

■ *Circular walks - North York Moors*
BOOK ONE - WESTERN MOORS
BOOK TWO - SOUTHERN MOORS
BOOK THREE - NORTHERN MOORS

■ *Circular walks - South Pennines*
WALKS IN BRONTE COUNTRY
WALKS IN CALDERDALE

■ *Hillwalking - Lake District*
OVER LAKELAND MOUNTAINS
OVER LAKELAND FELLS

80 DALES WALKS - an omnibus *(Cordee, Leicester)*

WALKING COUNTRY

HARROGATE
and the
WHARFE VALLEY

PUB WALKS

Valerie Yewdall

Illustrated by
Paul Hannon

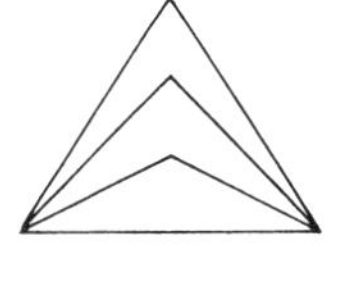

HILLSIDE

HILLSIDE
PUBLICATIONS
11 Nessfield Grove
Keighley
West Yorkshire
BD22 6NU

First published 1994

ISBN 1 870141 25 3

Whilst the author has walked and researched all the routes for the purposes of this guide, no responsibility can be accepted for any unforeseen circumstances encountered while following the walks. The publisher would, however, greatly appreciate any information regarding material changes to the routes, and any problems encountered.

Cover illustration: The Scotts Arms, Sicklinghall
Back cover:
Almscliff Crag; Harewood House; Knaresborough
(Paul Hannon/Big Country Photo Library)

Printed in Great Britain by
Carnmor Print and Design
95-97 London Road
Preston
Lancashire
PR1 4BA

CONTENTS

HARROGATE & THE WHARFE VALLEY

Location map showing starting points, walk numbers and major towns and villages

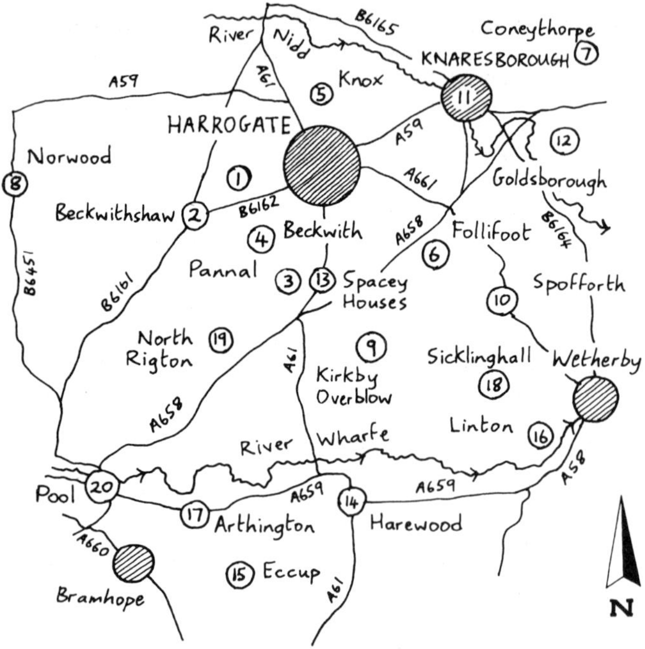

River Nidd
B6165
Coneythorpe
KNARESBOROUGH 7
A59
A61
Knox 5
11
HARROGATE
A59
12
Norwood
8
1
A661
Goldsborough
Beckwithshaw 2
B6162
Beckwith
A658
Follifoot
B6164
4
6
B6451
Pannal
3 13 Spacey Houses
B6161
10
Spofforth
North Rigton 19
9
Sicklinghall
Wetherby
A61
Kirkby Overblow
18
A658
Linton 16
River Wharfe
A58
Pool 20
A659
14
A659
17 Arthington
Harewood
A660
15 Eccup
Bramhope
A61
N

Rock gymnastics at Almscliff (not obligatory)

FOREWORD

Most people who walk in the countryside are aware of that great institution, the village pub. There is a very real pleasure in combining fresh air and exercise with the charms of a country inn, and this guidebook suggests 20 such opportunities.

The area between Harrogate and Harewood is largely unsung in walking terms, but those who constantly head off on long car journeys for the grander surrounds of the Dales or the Lakes would do well to sometimes look on their very doorstep. Many of the paths in this book are relatively seldom trodden, a great bonus as more folk take to the countryside. The easy nature of the walking is condusive to family outings, and most of the pubs welcome children (as long as they bring their parents!). Most of those featured have gardens and outdoor play areas, to boot.

The pubs visited - though varied in so many ways - fall into a similar group, being located as they are in what is generally accepted as a 'well to do' area of Yorkshire. You will be lucky to find a truly unspoilt village local - though the Gardener's at Bilton, where I've spent a happy hour or two, has so far avoided the pub planners. Equally, however, one is safe in the knowledge that there is nothing sub-standard to be encountered.

The vast majority of these walks can also be reached by bus, though one or two are rather tucked away. Some guides make a point of excluding walks not accessible by public transport, on the grounds that cars and pubs don't mix. This is based on an assumption that all people entering pubs are about to consume vast quantities of alcohol. Personally, I feel that most pub-users, and more importantly users of a book such as this, are well aware of the dangers of drinking and driving, and don't need a book publisher's sermon.

Finally, as a traditional beer enthusiast I encourage you non-drivers to sample any ales you find from smaller brewers. By all means enjoy your Tetleys, Youngers and Theakstons, but savour also the likes of Sam Smiths, Camerons, Vaux, and the minnows. One last thought - if you are visiting the pub first, don't forget the other bit - the walk!

Cheers!

Paul Hannon

INTRODUCTION

This is a book of walks for those who enjoy walking combined with a pub lunch. If one starts a walk at a pub it not only provides a place of refreshment, but a focal point of the walk and somewhere to park a car. Most publicans will have no objection to you leaving your car in their car park provided you have participated in their wares. It would be safer, and a courtesy, to ask before leaving your car.

The walks vary in length to suit all tastes and are comparatively easy. Nevertheless, boots and waterproofs are recommended.

I hope others may find as much pleasure and enjoyment in walking these routes as I have in compiling them.

Bon appetit, and put your best foot forward!

USING THIS GUIDE

Each walk is based on a particular hostelry, and sometimes a handy alternative is also mentioned. Opening times are included, though not carved in stone. Sundays are not included, as these are almost universally 12.00 till 3.00 and 7.00 till 10.30 (though some remain open for food and light refreshment throughout the day). In the precarious pub business, details can change overnight. A new licensee can have a drastic effect on a pub, for better or for worse; opening times, meals, beer range, and attitudes to walkers can all change. Don't blame us!

The use of an Ordnance Survey map is recommended in conjunction with the route description. All of the walks fall within either of two Pathfinder sheets (663, Harrogate, and 672, Harewood) at the scale of 1:25,000 (2½ inches to the mile). As these show all footpaths and field boundaries in detail, they are the most suitable to use. In addition, all the walks are covered on Sheet 104 of the 1:50,000 Landranger series. It is ideal for appraising the locations of the walks.

Each walk introduction gives details of the starting point, including grid reference, distance, relevant map, how to get there, availability of public transport, and the nature of the terrain.

SOME USEFUL ADDRESSES

Ramblers' Association
1/5 Wandsworth Road, London SW8 2XX
Tel. 071-582 6878

Harrogate Tourist Information
Royal Baths Assembly Rooms
Crescent Road, Harrogate HG1 2RR
Tel. 0423-525666

Knaresborough Tourist Information
35 Market Place, Knaresborough HG5 8AL
Tel. 0423-866886 (seasonal opening)

Otley Tourist Information
Council Offices, 8 Boroughgate, Otley LS21 3AH
Tel. 0943-465151

Campaign for Real Ale
34 Alma Road, St Albans, Herts AL1 3BW
Tel. 0727-867201

British Rail Tel. (Leeds) 0532-448133

Bus operators
Harrogate & District Travel Tel. 0423-566061

Yorkshire Rider (Leeds) Tel. 0532-451601

THE COUNTRY CODE

Respect the life and work of the countryside
Protect wildlife, plants and trees
Keep to public paths across farmland
Safeguard water supplies
Go carefully on country roads
Keep dogs under control
Guard against all risks of fire
Fasten all gates
Leave no litter - take it with you
Make no unnecessary noise
Leave livestock, crops and machinery alone
Use gates and stiles to cross fences, hedges and walls

HARROGATE

START *The Harrogate Arms, Crag Lane, Harrogate*
Grid Ref. 278542

DISTANCE *6 miles*

MAP *Pathfinder 663 - Harrogate*

ACCESS *From Harrogate take the B6162 to Harlow Car Gardens. After approximately a mile turn right into Crag Lane. Turn left after Harlow Car Gardens. Buses from the town centre run part way to the gardens.*

TERRAIN *Easy. Allow 3 hours at a leisurely pace to appreciate all the historic buildings.*

THE PUB

The Harrogate Arms is in a secluded setting hidden in the trees. It was previously the home of the Rowntree Chocolate family and it must have been an imposing residence. Note the old photograph of the Tewit Well on the left of the entrance.

Today there is a lively atmosphere with live entertainment and disco evenings. Children are welcome, and there is a garden. Lunches and evening meals are served at reasonable prices.

Opening hours
12.00-3.00, 6.00-11.00; all day in summer

Draught beers
Younger Scotch, No.3; Theakston XB

THE WALK

Walk back up the pub's entrance drive. Turn right at the top then left after the entrance to Pinewood Farm. Follow a track through a very pleasant wooded glade leading to a road. Proceed straight across to continue on the track through the wood to arrive at a 1914-1918 War Memorial.

You are now in the Valley Gardens and pass the bowling green and tennis courts to come to glorious flower beds leading to the entrance gate. Cross on the zebra crossing to the Royal Pump Room Museum noting the plaque on its wall.

Pass to the left of the Pump House (toilets on left if needed) coming to the next historical building of note - the Royal Baths, now a tourist information centre here.

To your left is the Royal Hall Theatre and the incongruous new Conference Centre. Turn right up Parliament Street, passing the Pump Room Inn to arrive at the top at Betty's Cafe and the War Memorial. Continue forward, follow the sunken way with the Stray on the right.

At the roundabout cross to Leeds Road and a sunken pathway running between horse chestnut trees leading to the historic Tewit Well.

The Tewit Well was the original source of remedial spring water to be found in Harrogate.

The Harrogate Arms

Captain William Slingsby of Bilton, a member of a famous Royalist family, was said to have discovered the well in 1571. His horse stumbled on the spring, which was circled by a flock of peewits or tewits, as they were called locally. The Captain had the area paved and walled and began to publicise what came to be known as the Tewit Well.

This well was the first to be described as a 'spa', thus named because it resembled the mineral wells at the town of Spa in Belgium. Many more wells were discovered, and Harrogate became known as the 'Queen of Watering Places'.

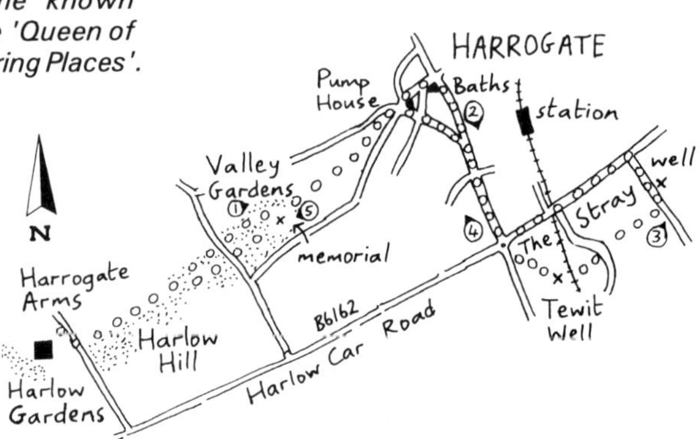

After an inspection turn back and right over the railway bridge, following the path to cross over St. James Drive. The open grassland of the Stray is on the left. Cross the next road to Slingsby Walk to reach Wedderburn House, noting again the information on the wall.

Turn left here to visit John's Well on the right. Cross back over the road and walk forward on the other side of the Stray back to the War Memorial. Turn right on the outward path to return to the centre and Valley Gardens. Retrace steps to the War Memorial noting the plaque of Bogs Field which contains 36 different mineral wells.

At the War Memorial take the lower path to the right leading through the wood, crossing a road and into the wood again to retrace steps back to Crag Lane. Turn left for Harlow Car Gardens and afternoon tea? If not, turn right then left, back to the Harrogate Arms.

HARROGATE

By the late 17th century visitors were coming to 'take the waters' in great numbers. The tiny hamlet grew into High and Low Harrogate, offering hospitality at the first inn to be built in 1687 - the Queen's Head, joined by 1700 by the Green Dragon and Royal Oak (later the Granby). Closely linked with the discovery of the mineral springs are the magnificent tree-lined spaces in the heart of the town - some 215 acres in all - the unspoilt Common of the Stray which gives Harrogate its distinctive character. This land was bequeathed by George III in 1770, to remain unenclosed for the pleasure of future generations. Harrogate is unique to have this vast area of unspoilt grassland in its centre which can never be built on.

John's Well or the Sweet Spa is situated on the Stray, on the left of the road leading to Wetherby. It was discovered by Dr. Michael Stanhope of York in 1631, and was reputed to exceed the Tewit water, if that was possible! The name derives from John Hardestie, who was the attendant there for many years until his death at 96. The waters certainly kept him alive, or was it something stronger?

During Victoria's reign Harrogate grew from strength to strength. In 1826, the first Harrogate Bath Hospital was built, catering for 300 patients, especially the poor. The Royal Pump Room once served 1500 glasses of sulphur water in a single morning! Baths in saline and sulphur water and heated mud were taken: visitors can still sample the water of the original sulphur well.

The increase of medical knowledge caused the decline of Harrogate as a spa, but today it is a centre of tourism, conferences, exhibitions and all kinds of cultural and sporting activities. The motto of its coat of arms means - 'to be of service' - a function which it fulfils admirably.

The Royal Pump Room Museum

2

BECKWITHSHAW

START *The Smith Arms, Beckwithshaw Grid ref. 268532*

DISTANCE *6 miles*

MAP *Pathfinder 663 - Harrogate*

ACCESS *Take the B6162 from Harrogate past Harlow Car Gardens. Beckwithshaw is at its junction with the B6161 Pool-Killinghall road. Buses from the town centre run part of the way here.*

TERRAIN *Easy, good clear tracks*

THE PUB

The Smith Arms is an old pub, dating back to 1860 when it was a blacksmith's shop - hence the name. At one time it was used as a school, and early this century it became a public house. The inside is panelled throughout, and note the beautiful carved oak settle.

Bar snacks are available and there is also a restaurant. A carvery buffet is available and open all day on Sunday. A pub with plenty of atmosphere and good food.

Opening hours
12.00-2.30, 5.30-11.00

Draught beers
John Smith Bitter
Ruddles County

THE WALK

Turn left when leaving the pub, passing the old school house dated 1865. Turn left opposite the cricket field, through a gate to Spring Hill Farm. Follow the good track round on the left of two woods. Just before the cattle-grid note the trees growing out of the rock in a most unusual way.

The track curves round to the right, leading round to Spring Hall Farm. Turn left after the cattle-grid to a gate by the farm buildings. At two gates, take the one on the right. Pass through another two gates. Ahead are wide views of rolling countryside.

The Smiths Arms, Beckwithshaw

Follow the wall on the left leading to a derelict farm. Pass through three gates. At the third gate bear right to another opening. Follow the line of telegraph poles to a ladder-stile at a wall corner. This leads into gorse and drops down to a road. Turn right over the bridge and Scargill Beck.

Turn right through a small gate at the Water Authority grounds. Head up the rough field to a gate at the top, leading to another gate at Long Liberty Farm and its access road.

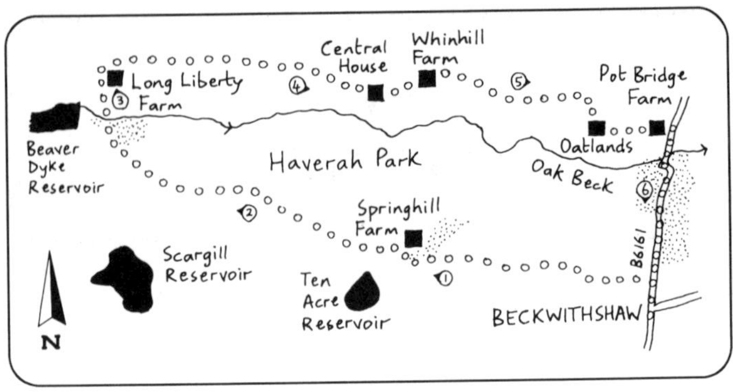

Go straight across the road and quickly right to follow the footpath sign on a rough lane leading to two gates. Follow the wall on the left to an enclosed way. At the gate at the end turn right towards Central House Farm.

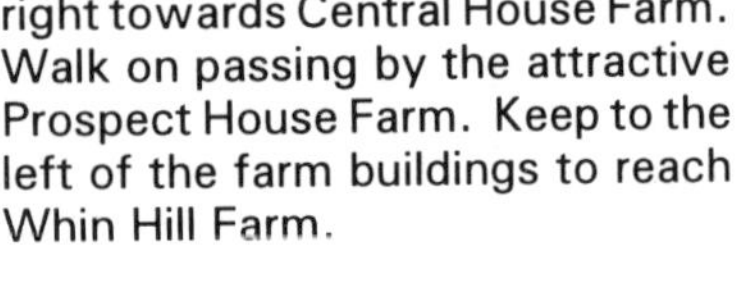

Walk on passing by the attractive Prospect House Farm. Keep to the left of the farm buildings to reach Whin Hill Farm.

After passing through two gates at the corner of a wood turn right with the wall on the right leading to Oatlands Farm, and further down the track Pot Bridge Farm and the main road. Turn right over the bridge and then up the road back to the Smiths Arms.

Beckwithshaw Church

3

PANNAL

START *The Black Swan, Pannal Grid ref. 299514*

DISTANCE *6 miles*

MAP *Pathfinder 663 - Harrogate*

ACCESS *1 mile off the A61 at Spacey Houses, 2 miles south of Harrogate. Bus service from the town centre.*

TERRAIN *Easy*

THE PUB

The Black Swan is a very up-market pub, and is beautifully appointed with antique furniture. Note the mounted Deeds of the Property over one of the open fireplaces when it was sold for £1,475.

There is a restaurant with an a la Carte menu. All the food is freshly cooked and most mouth-watering. They have an imaginative selection of sandwiches, choose from Yorkshire Tyke, Beside the Seaside, Fowl Play, Harvester and 'Fer thi sen!' All most appetizing and attractive.

Children are welcome, and there is a garden.

Opening hours
12.00-3.00, 6.00-11.00

Draught beers
Theakston Bitter, XB
Courage Directors
Ruddles County

THE WALK

Take the footpath sign to Pannal opposite the pub along the side of the Crimple Beck, on Malthouse Lane. Turn right over the footbridge, then left past the Old Maltings, the beck is now on the left. Pass the attractive duckpond to reach the main road.

Turn left over the bridge, then right to the church on the Ringway footpath. Go down the left-hand side of the church. Pass through a gate and over a stile at a double gate. Go straight forward through three stiles to the beck-side. Follow the fence round to the left away from the beck. After a stile turn right to the road.

The Black Swan, Pannal

Go straight across to a bridleway to Fulwith Mill Lane. Then go through a gate onto a narrow enclosed way to a small gate. Turn right then left into an open field and a gate. Head for the viaduct and two gates, take the one on the right. Continue forward, ignoring the bridleway to Follifoot Road.

Pass through a gate onto a farm road. Continue straight up the hill past Fulwith Grange, to the top and round to the left past imposing detached villas to the main road. Turn left a few yards, cross the road and follow the Ringway down Stone Rings Lane.

At the end turn right over the stile into an enclosed way. Take the large metal gate leading to a narrow way leading to a stile and a narrow enclosed way, turning right on the side of the beck to arrive at a road. Turn left to a junction, and here turn right on Green Lane. Turn left on the footpath to Yew Tree Lane.

Follow the hedge round the sports field to the road. Turn right briefly, then left at a footpath sign on a narrow, enclosed way. Over the wooden bridge into a field, here go right to a stile, and turn right to the road.

Turn left to the Squinting Cat (see WALK 4). Turn left at the road junction on Hill Top Lane to turn left again almost immediately on the Ringway path. Turn right over a stile in a hedge, over the next stile, with the hedge now on the left. Over the next stile, the hedge is now on the right.

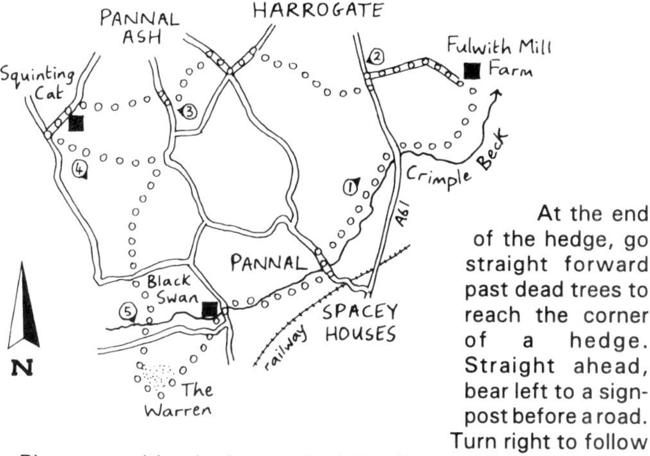

At the end of the hedge, go straight forward past dead trees to reach the corner of a hedge. Straight ahead, bear left to a sign-post before a road. Turn right to follow the Ringway, with a hedge on the left. Over a stile into the field and gate ahead. Bear right to a stile in the corner to the next stile. Go straight on, with a hedge on the right to the stile in the corner.

Go straight ahead to a fence corner and gate and stile into a narrow way leading to a road. Turn right and quickly left at Southlands on the Ringway path, with a wall on the right to cross a wooden bridge which leads to a road.

For a quick return, turn left down the road to the Black Swan. Otherwise, cross the road and slightly right, through a gate into woods. Climb to the top and through a gate, turn left outside the wood. Turn left at the bottom on the Ringway to a gate and a stile, with a hedge on the left to reach a minor road. Go straight across to reach the next road. Turn left to the Black Swan.

4

BECKWITH

START *The Squinting Cat, Beckwith   Grid ref. 287525*

DISTANCE *3½ miles*

MAP *Pathfinder 663 - Harrogate*

ACCESS *Take the Otley road out of the town, and shortly turn left along Pannal Ash Road. At the roundabout, keep straight on up Whinney Lane. A bus service from the town centre runs near the start.*

TERRAIN *Fields and lanes*

THE PUB

The Squinting Cat dates from the 17th century when it was a farm. The owner was a woman with a squint who owned a cat, I was informed, so it wasn't the cat that squinted.

The pub has plenty of character with open fires, the former barn has been left with its high beam and note the block and tackle in the rafters used for lifting.

It is open seven days a week for lunch and evening meals. There is a wide choice of food with an Italian menu and a salad bar. There is a rear garden and barbecue area.

Opening hours
12.00-3.00, 5.30-11.00, and all day Saturday

Draught beers
Tetley Bitter

THE WALK

On leaving the pub, turn left up to the road and then left down Hill Top Lane. After 100 yards turn right on the footpath which is a broad track between hedges leading down to the beck.

Cross the footbridge on the right and up to a fence. Bear right, through a fence and up to a gate in the corner to a gate on the left. Here turn left to continue to a road.

Turn right briefly, then left at the side of Field Head Farm on a diverted track. Cross over the stile in the corner and follow the fence down on the right to a stile at the bottom. Go down to Alder Carr House Farm, and down the access road.

The Squnting Cat,
Beckwith

Turn left at the road to the main road, turning right past Highfields, turning left after The Croft. This is an enclosed narrow way leading to a footbridge leading up Fall Lane to the main road. Turn left on Hill Top Lane.

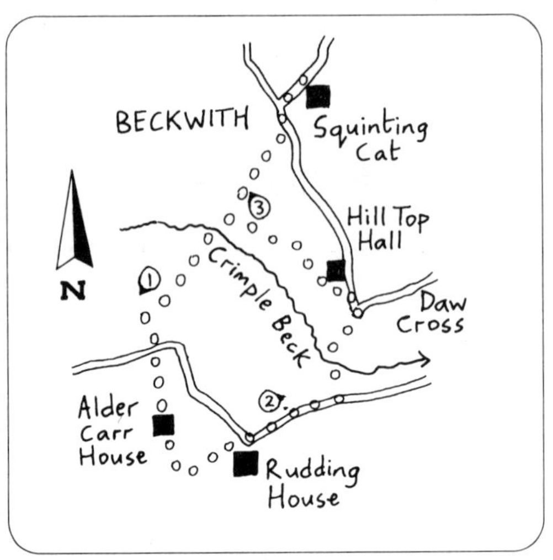

Take the footpath sign at Cobler Hill House on the left. Turn left at the farm at the top. Through three gates, turn right round the farm buildings to the gate at the bottom. Go straight forward to another gate.

Bear left to a waymarked stile over a ditch to the next stile and signpost. Turn right to Lund House Green, up the field on the outward track, to reach the road. Turn left, then right, back to the Squinting Cat.

An old water pump at the Squinting Cat

KNOX

START *The Knox Arms, Knox, Harrogate*
Grid ref. 299575

DISTANCE *4½ miles*

MAP *Pathfinder 663 - Harrogate*

ACCESS *Off the A61 Harrogate-Ripon Road. Turn uphill at the new roundabout by the Little Wonder Pub. Turn left at the Dragon pub onto Bilton Road, and left again at Crab Lane. Knox is served by the Bilton bus from the town centre. Killinghall (mid-walk) is also served by Ripon and Pateley Bridge buses from Harrogate.*

TERRAIN *Fields and lanes, some road work.*

THE PUB

The Knox Arms was converted from a farmhouse by Theakstons Brewery in 1985. It is very attractively set out in pine in the original barn.

There is a good choice of food from the separate food bar. On the Sunday of my visit it was extremely busy.

Opening hours
11.30-3.00, 5.30-11.00; all day Friday and Saturday

Draught beers
Theakston Mild, Bitter, XB

THE WALK

Turn right down Knox Lane to reach the bridge at the bottom, this is Spruisty Bridge and ford, on Oak Beck. Go straight across and up Knox Mill Bank. Turn left, then through the snicket between the houses leading to a field. Go straight ahead and over the stile at the field corner, heading for Spruisty Hill Farm and a small white gate. Follow the wall on the right to another gate to a further stile leading to the access road.

The Knox Arms, Knox

Turn right up the access road. Keep left of the farm at Spruisty Hall, through two gates, and bear right at a stile left of the buildings at Spruisty Grange Farm. Turn right at a sign between the buildings, through a gate to a stile on the left. Follow the hedge on the left to the bottom to cross a beck and fence. Follow a hedge on the left to a stile in the corner, go straight ahead to a stile in the hedge. Bear right to a stile in the corner onto a lane.

Turn right on the lane, through the gate ahead to a field. Proceed down the side of the hedge on the left to a hidden stile over the wall at the bottom, to a stile in a double fence. Turn right to the old Nidd Bridge, and go under the modern road bridge to follow the river Nidd upstream. Turn left up the side of the fence leading to Malt Kiln Farm to reach the access road.

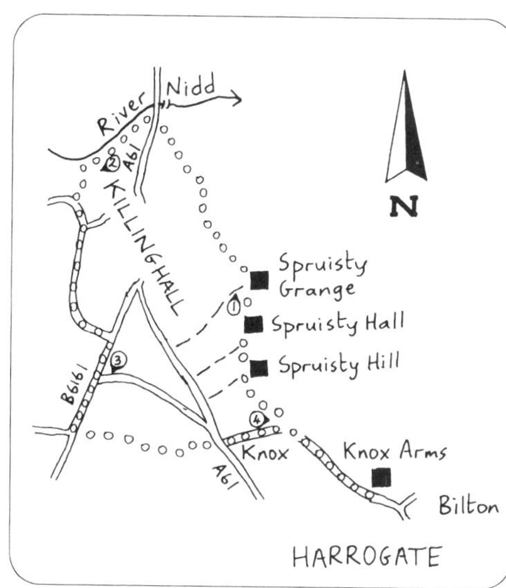

Turn left to the farm. Go right at the junction down Crag Lane to the B6161 road at Killinghall school. Turn right passing Grainbeck Lane (do not go down it) to turn left at High Warren at the roadsign for Hampsthwaite and Birstwith.

Proceed down the field with the hedge on the right to the bottom. Cross the fence and ditch, here turning right to a tricky section between ditch and fence to a small gate leading to a track. Turn left to the signpost.

Turn right on the Ringway path to the main road. Cross the road and on Knox Mill Lane, leading to Spruisty Bridge again. Cross the bridge and back to the pub.

Spruisty Bridge, Oak Beck

6

FOLLIFOOT

START *The Radcliffe Arms, Follifoot Grid ref. 340526*
or The Lascelles Arms, Follifoot Grid ref. 341525

DISTANCE *7 miles*

MAP *Pathfinder 663 - Harrogate*

ACCESS *Off the A658, 2½ miles south-east of Harrogate. Served by the Harrogate-Wetherby bus.*

TERRAIN *Easy, good paths, very pleasant section through woods by the river Nidd.*

THE PUBS

The RADCLIFFE ARMS takes its name from a Lord Radcliffe who owned land in this area. He died intestate, so the name died out.

The pub is old, and very attractive. It is open seven days a week for lunches and dinners. In the summer barbecues are held at the rear in the ample car park.

Opening hours 11.00-3.00, 5.30-11.00

• • • • • • • • • • • • • • •

The LASCELLES ARMS is a very pleasant pub on the main street, with a cosy bar. Food is served at normal times. There is also a beer garden, and families are welcome.

Opening hours 11.30-3.00, 5.30-11.00

Draught beers Samuel Smith Old Brewery Bitter

THE WALK

Leaving the Radcliffe Arms, turn left, passing the impressive Rudding Arch on the left. Pass the church and take the footpath sign to Rudding Lane, through the churchyard. This descends the field to the A658.

Cross over with care and follow the marked path to the edge of the wood (The Carrs). Turn right, and keeping the wall on the left, continue round the edge of the wood. Cross the stile and continue with the wall on the left, until a stile is reached at the access road to Rudding Dower.

Turn right, before reaching the main road, and turn right down the lane towards Ducks Nest Farm. Take the first of two gates on the left, and the path through the fields with the wall on the right. Pass through the small gate at the bottom into the wood. Cross Crimple Beck by stepping stones and up to the A661 road.

The Lascelles Arms, Follifoot

Turn right along the Harrogate-Wetherby road, crossing a bridge and up to the footpath sign to the Ringway path, leading to Rudfarlington Farm. Continue down the farm track to open fields with a hedge on the left. As the track fades, continue forward in the same direction enclosed by hedgerows, leaving to turn half-right across the field to a footpath sign by a solitary tree. Pass through the hedge and follow the farm track to the road.

The Radcliffe Arms, Follifoot

Turn right, passing the garden centre on the left and many attractive houses to a junction with the B6163 at Calcutt, and the Union pub (see WALK 11). Here turn left and take the footpath to Spittlecroft. At the next footpath sign for Grimbald Bridge turn right. Go through the wood with the river Nidd on the left. This is a very pleasant section, especially when the bluebells and garlic are in flower.

Continue downstream for some distance. When the houses finish take the stile to the fenced track returning to the riverside in the wood. An excellent riverside walk follows, climbing to a fence at a caravan site. Follow the fence to its demise. Turn right on the road through the site. At the site top turn right towards a toilet block and right again down the road with the hedge on the left (up one side of the site and down the other).

Continue on the path into the wood with the river now down on your right. At a fork in the path, bear left. At the end of Birkham Wood re-cross the A658 road to re-enter the wood on the other side. Keep to the path through the wood to emerge into a field. Turn right on the field edge, then left on the track to Plompton Hall.

Turn right, then left passing the ancient hall and coach house dated 1760. Continue on the road with the fence on the right (ignoring the left fork) leading round to East Lodge.

The pleasure grounds at Plompton Rocks were laid out by Daniel Lascelles. Comprising about 23 acres, huge grey rocks are mixed with shrubs, flowers and evergreens. At the foot of the rocks is a lake covering about seven acres, which adds greatly to the beauty of the scenery. The grounds are open at weekends and Bank Holidays, and on paying my small entry fee I met the owner, Edward De Plumpton Hunter, last descendant of the line.

The main Plompton Rock is a most singular edifice, rising in an irregular circular mass to a height of 24 feet, with a circumference of over 90 feet. The top is crowned with a mass of heather growing in the peat. Through one side is a large perforation, in which is a rock basin. The basin is about two feet deep, and about four feet in its diameter.

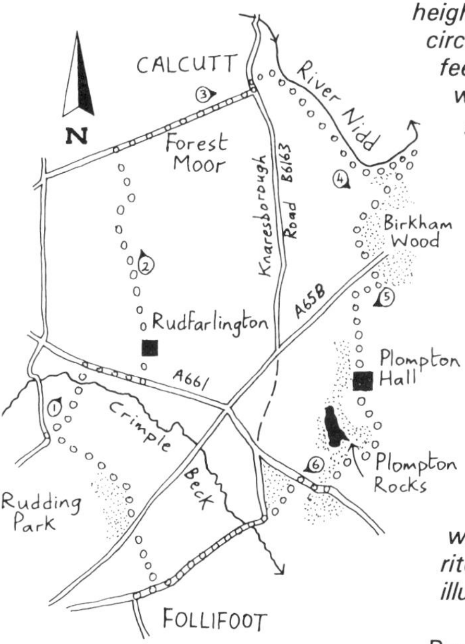

This natural formation has had some form of connection with Druidical worship rites. The main rock is illustrated on Page One.

Pass the lodge, entering Plompton Park and go down to the main road. Turn right down the road, and just before Brown Hill Wood seek out a concealed stile on the the left. Continue through the field with the wall on the right on the edge of the wood. At the field corner cross the stile back to the road, turn left to cross the bridge and follow the road back to Follifoot.

PLOMPTON HALL

Plompton gets its name from 'plump' meaning a woody place. A clump of trees is still called a plump in Yorkshire. 'ton' means a town. The ancient manor of Plumpton was described in the Domesday Book. It was bequeathed to Sir Robert Plumpton in return for his services as Constable of Knaresborough Castle and Chief Forester, until his death in 1406. The office was passed down to the next generation until the end of the reign of Henry VI.

After the decease of the last heir in 1749, who died without leaving issue, the family became extinct. The estate passed to a Benedictine nun, who sold the estate to Daniel Lascelles, and now belongs to the Earl of Harewood. Daniel Lascelles pulled down the old mansion, and commenced building a new one, but he purchased the Goldsborough estate and took up residence there instead. The unfinished building was dismantled: it stood to the south-west of the present farmhouse, and the site is marked by two pillars of limestone.

Plompton Hall Farm

CONEYTHORPE

START *The Tiger Inn, Coneythorpe   Grid ref. 394590*

DISTANCE *7 miles*

MAP *Pathfinder 663 - Harrogate*

ACCESS *On A59 Knaresborough to York Road, turn left to Flaxby and left to Coneythorpe. Served by the Knaresborough-Ripon/ Boroughbridge bus.*

TERRAIN *Easy, level tracks through pastures*

THE PUB

The Tiger Inn is pleasantly situated in the rural village of Coneythorpe. It overlooks the village green with its ancient water pump and attractive brick houses.

The pub has a restaurant as well as home cooked bar snacks. There is a homely atmosphere with an open fire, which was much appreciated as the day we did this walk it was snowing.

Opening hours 12.00-2.30, 7.00-11.00 (closed Mon lunch)

Draught beers
Tetley Bitter
Theakston Bitter
occasional guest beer

The village pump

THE WALK

On leaving the pub, walk up the road passing the village pump on the right. At the road junction, keep to the main road. At the bend and just above Clareton Moor Farm, take the footpath sign on the left. Follow the track round to a gate and continue down the track, through fields with the hedge on the left.

When the hedge finishes follow the telegraph poles. Bear half-right down a wide track leading towards The Hollies, crossing stiles and fields en route. Before reaching the farm, pass through the hedge and turn left to follow the hedge. On reaching the track at the bottom of the field, turn left, and quickly right to follow the blue arrow. Follow the wide track down the field edge with the hedge on the left.

Tiger Inn, Coneythorpe

Pass through a gate into an enclosed path, leading to another field and passing a solitary tree on the right with a good view of Knaresborough ahead. Follow the track down to Hopewell House and straight forward round the back of the farm leading into fields with the fence on the left.

Continue on through a gateway into the next field and continue with the hedge on the left. Keep to the field edge up to a white gate, passing through and leading to a lane. Here turn left as indicated and follow it down past Bridge Farm, with Knaresborough Lagoon on the left.

Take the stile on the left before crossing the disused railway bridge and follow the signposted track through the gate, across the fields with the lagoon and its bird-life on the left. On reaching the water's edge, cross over the stile onto the road. Turn left down the lane passing large, disused greenhouses and coming to the main road.

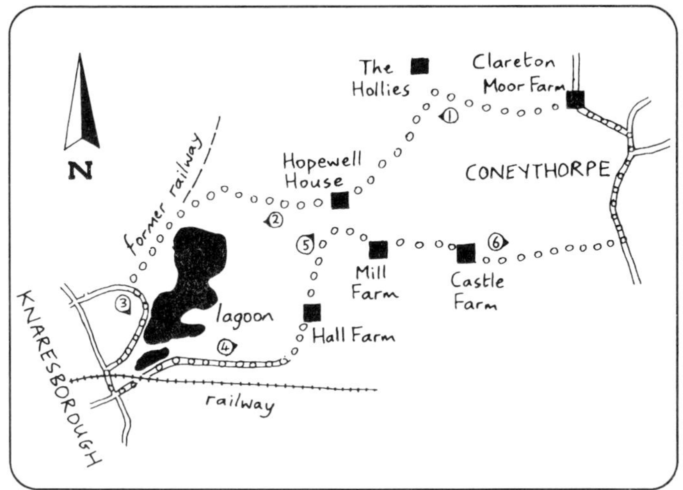

Turn left under the bridge on to Halfpenny Lane and the crossroads. Turn left on Park Lane. Continue on this lane passing Forest School, on under a bridge and passing a rugby field. Continue along the lane towards Hall and Hopewell Farms. Pass through the pig-farmyard and continue to where the road turns to Hopewell Farm. Here leave the road and turn right on a rough track passing Tyeralea House and then between a disused farm.

A good, broad green track follows through fields leading to a gate. Pass through and continue forward with the fence on the right, to another gate leading to Castle Farm. Turn right, then left through the farmyard to follow the farm access track leading to the main road.

Turn left down Shorthill Lane back into Coneythorpe and the Tiger Inn.

8

NORWOOD

START *The Sun Inn, Norwood Grid ref. 207538*

DISTANCE *3 miles*

MAP *Pathfinder 663 - Harrogate*

ACCESS *On the B6451 Otley to Pateley Bridge road*

TERRAIN *Easy, can be muddy in wet weather*

THE PUB

The Sun Inn is very old and has plenty of character with its stone walls and large open fireplaces. It was built in 1770 and is situated in the picturesque Washburn Valley, 10 minutes from Harrogate and Otley. Breakfasts, lunches, afternoon tea and evening meals are served. Summer barbecues are held each Friday and Saturday evening in the beer garden, and there is live entertainment. There is a games room and a children's play area.

The pub has an extensive menu to choose from, the portions are ample and the food flavoursome.

Opening hours 11.00-11.00

Draught beers Younger Scotch; Theakston Bitter

The Sun Inn, Norwood

THE WALK

On leaving the pub turn left and pass through the farm buildings to a gate and a stile. Aim for the next stile in the wall in front, and follow the footpath along the left-hand side of the wall at the top of the field. Continue in the same direction, through stiles until the path drops down and crosses a concealed footbridge. From here head right to Brown Bank Farm.

Pass through the gate opposite and with the farm on the left. Turn left in front of the farmhouse and continue to two gates, take the one on the right. Continue with the wall on the left and through another stile. The track veers right to approach the fine old property of East End Manor. The route goes through a gate to pass in front of the manor, then to the left following arrows.

Drop down the field and after passing a red-roofed building on the left, turn right to reach the enclosed track to a disused farm. Take the gate to its right and follow the wall on the left down to a gate at the dam of Beaver Dyke Reservoir. Cross between the reservoirs, and turn left with the reservoir wall on the left to rise up the track to a gate, and another disused farm building.

Drop down to a marked gate to cross the beck and up to a signpost to Norwood. Turn left up the enclosed way to a gate. Turn right to follow the wall on the left to join an enclosed track to reach Bank End Farm. Keep in the same direction to a marked stile in the corner, on to the next stile and gate ahead.

Skirt around the marshy section to the stile ahead at a ditch. Turn left and up the field, bearing to the right towards the farm and the Sun Inn.

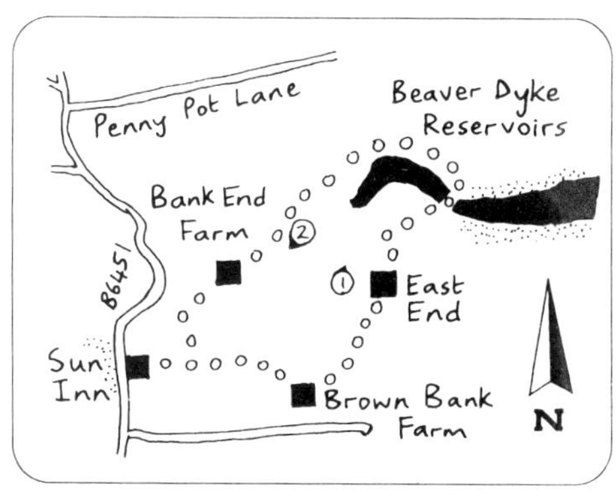

9

KIRKBY OVERBLOW

START *Star & Garter Inn, Kirkby Overblow Grid ref. 325493*
or Shoulder of Mutton, Kirkby Overblow

DISTANCE *7½ miles*

MAP *Pathfinder 672 - Harewood*

ACCESS *South of Harrogate, off the A658. Served by Wetherby-Harrogate schoolday bus.*

TERRAIN *Very easy, on good paths over rolling countryside*

THE WALK

When leaving the Star & Garter or Shoulder of Mutton proceed east down Barrowby Lane. At the triangle of grass and two large beech trees turn left over the cattle-grid. Immediately turn right along the back of some new houses. Pass through a gate, continuing with the fence on the right. Turn right through a gate, now with the fence on the left. Cross over a stile and follow a faint path to the corner of a wall.

Continue with the wall on the left and over a stile. Cross over the wall at the steps, now the wall is on the right leading into a wood. Go straight forward through a small gate at the end of the wood, and continue in the same direction with the hedge on the right leading into High Lane.

Continue on the lane to Fox Heads Farm, here turning right to a quarry. Follow Fox Heads Lane to emerge onto the road at Sicklinghall (a detour left leads to the Scotts Arms, see WALK 18). Go straight across the road on the footpath marked to East

Keswick. Follow the fence on the left round to a gate, and at the next stile turn right without crossing it, leading to a road (Paddock House Lane).

Turn left down the road. Before Paddock House Farm at the bottom, turn right and continue forward to another road at Kearby Town End. Turn right. At the road junction (the house on the corner was a pub until recent times) turn left. At the bend in the road look for a hidden stile in the wall. Cross the field diagonally, over a stile heading for three buildings ahead.

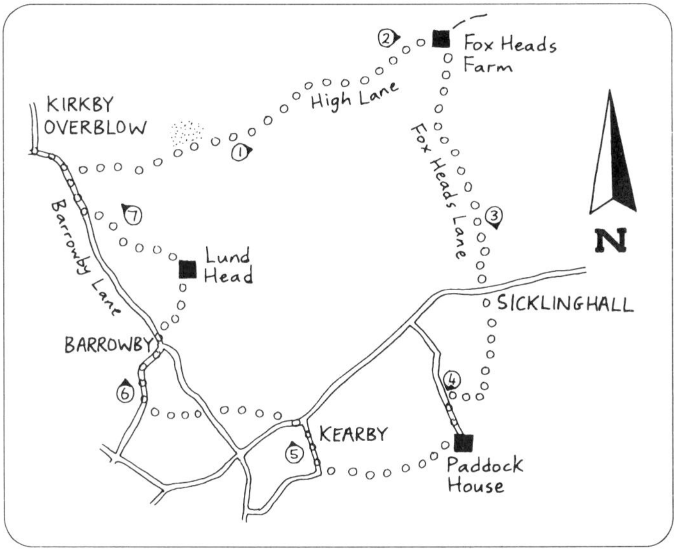

Pass round Kearby Methodist church onto the road. Go straight across the road and over the cattle-grid leading to a driveway, through a white gate dropping down to a road. Turn right up the hill to Barrowby, passing the old Manor.

At the road junction turn left, after 50 yards turn right on Lund Head Lane leading to Marsh Lane (a track). Turn left up onto a narrow hedged way leading onto the road. Turn right to return to Kirkby Overblow.

THE PUBS? see overleaf....

THE STAR & GARTER is warm and welcoming. I went to a Burns Night here when Haggis and Neeps were piped in by a kilted Scot and a recital of a Robbie Burns' poem. All this was free and also they provide a free buffet at Christmas! What more could you ask? The food is good and you can be sure of a friendly reception. Lunches and evening meals are provided.

Note the inscription on the sign 'Honi soit qui mal y pens' meaning 'The shame be his who thinks badly of it'. The Order of the Garter was founded by Edward III in 1348, and comprised of the sovereign and his knights, and this was their motto. It derived from the King tying to his leg a garter dropped by a lady at a banquet. Henceforth the motto was inscribed on the blue garter worn by a knight of the Order on the left leg below the knee.

Opening hours 11.00-11.00

Draught beers Cameron Bitter; Tetley Bitter

Star & Garter,. Kirkby Overblow

Kirkby Overblow was mentioned in the Domesday Book. It took its name from the ore blowers when the area was rich in iron deposits in the Middle Ages. In 1302 its name was recorded as Kirkby Orblowers. The village once had a moated hall which was burnt by the Royalists during the Civil War. All Saints church is a lovely building in the heart of the village.

THE SHOULDER OF MUTTON dates back to 1740 when it was a brewhouse. It has great character with oak beams. Look out for the grandfather clock, carved settle and coaching lights. When I visited it prior to Christmas the inn was most attractively decorated.

Home-cooked lunches are available daily except Mondays, and evening meals are served daily. There is a spacious garden at the rear.

Opening hours 12.00-3.00, 6.00-11.00

Draught beers Tetley Bitter; Theakston Bitter

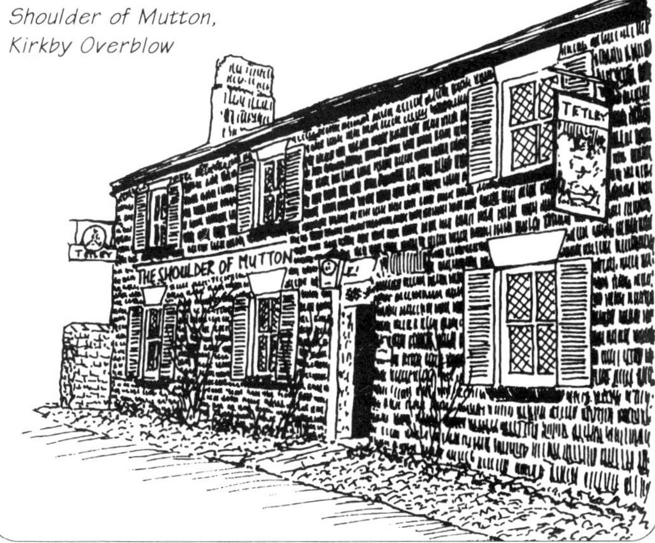

Shoulder of Mutton, Kirkby Overblow

10

SPOFFORTH

START *King William IV, Spofforth Grid ref. 362513*

DISTANCE *7 miles*

MAP *Pathfinder 663 - Harrogate*

ACCESS *On A661 Wetherby-Harrogate road. Served by the Harrogate-Wetherby bus.*

TERRAIN *Riverside and good tracks.*

THE PUB

William IV reigned from 1765 to 1837 and was known as the Sailor King or 'Silly Billy'. He served in the Royal Navy from 1778 to 1790. He had ten illegitimate children by the Irish actress Dorothea Jordan before his marriage, but no legal issue. William was succeeded by his niece, Queen Victoria.

One can see the pub dates back a long way. It was originally two cottages and later converted into a pub. The horse tethers are still to be seen outside for the use of travellers on horseback. Inside there is an unusual collection of cigarette cards recording the last surviving locomotives of the steam age.

The pub provides accommodation, lunches and evening meals, every day except Monday. The food is home made, attractively served and reasonably priced. There is also a beer garden.

Opening hours
12.00-3.00, 6.00-11.00

Draught beers
Vaux Bitter, Samson

There are two alternative starting pubs

THE CASTLE, another old building.

Opening hours 11.30-3.00, 5.30-11.00, and all day Saturday
Draught beers Tetley Bitter, Mild

THE RAILWAY, which is listed in the 1994 Good Beer Guide.

Opening hours 11.30-3.00, 5.30-11.00
Draught beers Samuel Smith Old Brewery Bitter, Museum Ale

THE WALK

On leaving the pub turn left to the main road. Turn left, passing Spofforth Castle on the right, to reach the main road and the Castle Inn. Turn left down Harrogate Road. Pass the church and over the bridge. Take the footpath on the left to follow Crimple Beck for 1 ½ miles up to the road. At the road turn right without going on it, and follow round the field edge with a wall on the left leading to the A661 Harrogate-Wetherby road.

Turn right and then left to Plompton Rocks (open to visitors, for a small admission fee: see WALK 6). Pass between the lodges. At the fork before Plompton Hall, turn right. Pass left of High Grange onto a broad track through the field. Pass to the right of Loxley Farm into Braham Wood and onto a concrete track to Throstle Nest Farm.

King William IV, Spofforth

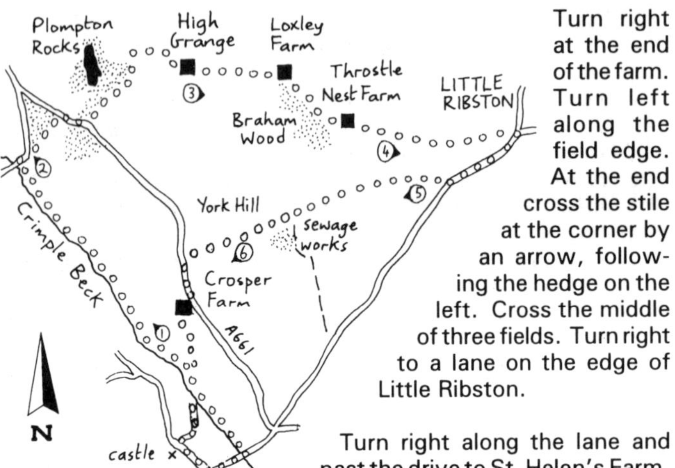

Turn right at the end of the farm. Turn left along the field edge. At the end cross the stile at the corner by an arrow, following the hedge on the left. Cross the middle of three fields. Turn right to a lane on the edge of Little Ribston.

Turn right along the lane and past the drive to St. Helen's Farm, take the next turn right at a sign onto a broad track to a sewage works. Exit at a gate, over a ditch and forward to the Water Authority sign. Here turn through the gate and follow the hedge on the left. Follow round the field edge, turning right to drop down to the main road.

Turn left to Crosper Farm, then through its entrance between the buildings. Follow the fence on the left, round a large rock to a stile at the bottom. Follow the hedge on the right: half-way along is a concealed way through, over a ditch. Aim diagonally across the field for the church. Follow the beck to a small bridge, and soon cross to another tiny bridge at the former mill, onto Mill Lane. At the top turn left to finish.

The Castle, Spofforth

SPOFFORTH CASTLE

William de Percy came to this country from Normandy in 1067. A favourite of William the Conqueror, he was granted 86 Lordships of York, including Spofforth. He established his headquarters here and built a manor house, of which nothing remains. The castle dates from the 13th century.

In 1309 Henry de Percy moved the family seat to Northumberland. From then onwards Spofforth's significance declined. It was last used as a residence in 1604. Oliver Cromwell was responsible for much of the castle's destruction. Some of the castle stone was used for building the nearby homes, but much of the original castle remains to be seen and is certainly worth a visit.

The nearby Manor House had problems with a smoking chimney, and two cannonballs were found lodged in it! Once again Oliver Cromwell was to blame as he missed his target - the castle - and hit the chimney of the Manor House.

Though restored in 1855, much earlier work remains in All Saints church. Inside is the figure of a knight, a 14th century monument to Sir Robert de Plompton.

11

KNARESBOROUGH

START *Mother Shipton's Inn, Knaresborough Grid ref. 350564*

DISTANCE *8 miles or 4 miles*

MAP *Pathfinder 663 - Harrogate*

ACCESS *Off the A658 to Calcutt, situated at the bottom of the hill by the bridge. Knaresborough is linked with Harrogate by bus and train.*

TERRAIN *Easy paths, with a very pleasant riverside route through woods*

THE PUB

Mother Shipton's Inn is 400 years old, formerly a farmhouse and a gem of antiquity. The refectory table where we dined once belonged to Guy Fawkes, and came from Scotton Hall, where he lived in 1592. Note the original oak panelling, settle and the open fireplace. There is a good collection of horse brasses, guns and old prints.

It is a good venue for walkers, cyclists and all travellers appreciating home cooked food served at lunchtime and in the evening. There is a family room and a beer garden

Opening hours
12.00-3.00, 5.30-11.00

Draught beers
Theakston Bitter; Younger Scotch, No.3; guest beer

Mother Shipton's Inn, Knaresborough

Directly behind the pub is the entrance to Mother Shipton's Cave, where she is believed to have been born in the reign of Henry VII. She foretold the future with amazing accuracy. When she died she was buried at Clifton near York, and a stone was erected bearing the following inscription:-

Here lies she who never ly'd,
Whose skill often has been try'd,
Her prophecies shall survive,
And keep her name alive

Near her cave is one of the strongest and most celebrated petrifying springs in the kingdom. The water of the well is so cold that anything dropped in quickly turns to stone. Various objects are on view, all turned to stone. DON'T FALL IN THE WELL!

THE WALK

On leaving the pub, turn right up the hill for 300 yards. Cross the road and take the footpath signed to Wetherby Road. Pass Spittlecroft, originally a hospital for lepers, founded in very early times. On arrival at the interesting house - Eden Roc - take the footpath to the right of the building, leading to a narrow enclosed way. Turn right at the signpost to Calcutt, the main road and the Union pub.

THE UNION is a favourite with sportsmen - a cricket field is adjacent and the Nidd just below. Bar lunches are served every day except Thursdays, with reasonably priced food on offer.

Opening times 12.00-3.00, 6.00-11.00; and all day Fri and Sat

Draught beers Marston Bitter and Pedigree

From the Union walk down the road opposite, Forest Moor Road. After 200 yards turn off right at the Ringway footpath sign. This is a good track, soon turning left and passing over two stiles into open fields. Follow the track on the field bottom, close to the hedge on the left. Leave at the signposted corner, crossing the stream and in the same direction diagonally across the field to reach the railway crossing - STOP - listen, and cross with care.

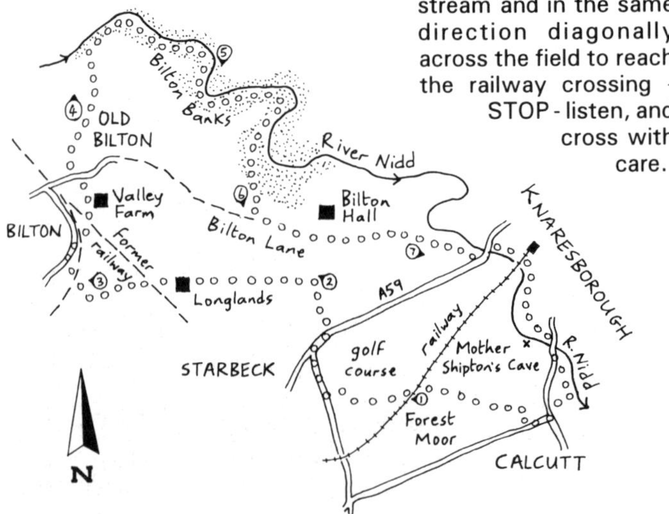

Take the path round the edge of the golf course, passing through trees, then bearing right, then left to emerge onto the road. Turn right up to the junction at the top. Turn right on the A59 York Road for approximately 200 yards. Turn left where signposted towards Bilton Hall nursing home. This is where you must decide which walk to do. The short one keeps on towards the hall.

For the main walk, turn left after 400 yards at the sign posted to Woodfield Lane, keeping the hedge on the right. Cross the stile with the hedge now on the left. After two fields cross the milk churn stile, and continue with the hedge on the left, across fields to Longlands Farm.

Follow the marked route down to a disused railway bridge. Cross over and take a path across the field in front, bearing slightly right. Cross the field to reach the wood. Turn right and follow the path down with the houses and hedge on the left. Cross the beck at the bottom and follow the path with the beck on the right. Cross the stile up to the old railway's cinder track.

Cross straight over and down some steps, through a stile to follow the beck to join a farm track by a footpath sign and gate. Valley Farm is on the right. Walk forward on the wide track to the Gardener's Arms.

THE GARDENER'S ARMS at Old Bilton is an old country pub providing home-made dishes - 'Steak 'n Stout Pie' - being the speciality of the house. It is a popular rendezvous for walkers. Next door is a small brewery - Franklins was started in 1980 in the early days of small brewery revivals. Its survival today makes it one of the long-established 'micros'.

Opening hours
12.00-3.00,
6.00-11.00

Draught beers
Samuel Smith
Old Brewery Bitter

The Gardener's Arms
Old Bilton

Take the footpath sign to the Nidd Gorge to the left of the pub. Cross the beck and up to Woodside Farm. Take the gate to the right into an enclosed track leading to an open field with the hedge on the right. Cross the field corner, there becoming enclosed again. Pass down through the wood (ignoring the left-hand fork), taking the path down to the riverside.

Turn right and continue downstream with the river Nidd on the left for a good mile. This is a very pleasant section following the river towards Knaresborough. At one point the path climbs into the wood, but soon returns to the riverside.

Ignore the wooden footbridge and continue on the riverside until the path climbs up through the wood high above the river. Continue through the top of the wood with fields on the right. Finally merging with a wide track, again passing along the top of the wood, and eventually crossing a stile into a field to reach Bilton Lane.

Turn left following the Ringway footpath sign and continue on the lane to the road. You are now back on the access road to Bilton Hall nursing home, where the shorter option is joined. Cross over at Bilton Hall onto the enclosed track (Ringway sign) leading into a field. Keep to the field side, with the hedge on the left. This is where we saw deer, so keep a look-out. Exit through a stile at the bottom corner.

At the sign take the Conyngham Hall Trail down to the river (Conyngham Hall is an 18th century mansion). Turn right to follow the river once again, and then up onto the main road at Knaresborough Bridge.

If you are willing to pay £3.65 you can walk through the grounds of Mother Shipton's Cave - at one time part-owned by 'celebrity' Paul Daniels - and back to the inn. Otherwise cross the bridge and turn right to walk on the opposite bank of the river.

Although on a road, this is a pleasant route, with many interesting houses built into the rocks, also an opportunity for ice-cream, afternoon tea or toilet stop, if required. Emerge onto the main road at the Half Moon Inn. Cross over the bridge to return to Mother Shipton's Inn.

On the return journey, look out for the 'House in the Rock', high on the hillside overlooking the river Nidd. This is well worth a visit, if you have the time and energy. There are a great many steps to climb before you reach a tiny door to the house carved out of the rock 200 years ago.

It is owned by Nancy Buckle and has been in the same family since 1770, when with chisel and hammer it was cut out of the rock. Nancy has no 'mod.cons.' - no toilet, bathroom, hot water, or telephone, and for this reason the council is condemning it as unsuitable for habitation.

This seems a great pity as Nancy is clean and healthy and happy in her home, and is determined to fight to remain where she is. 200 babies have been born in the house and survived! It may lack amenities but certainly not individuality. For £1 you can look around Nancy's unique home and judge for yourself.

Knaresborough Castle is situated high on a promontory above sandstone cliffs falling to the river Nidd. Its remains date from the early 14th century. It also overlooks a much more recent structure, that nevertheless forms an integral part of the local scene, namely the elegant railway viaduct.

Knaresborough Castle

12

GOLDSBOROUGH

START *Bay Horse Inn, Goldsborough Grid ref. 382562*

DISTANCE *7½ miles*

MAP *Pathfinder 663 - Harrogate*

ACCESS *At the terminal of the A658 with the A59 to York, turn right for one mile. The Knaresborough-Ripon/Boroughbridge bus runs nearby. Little Ribston (mid-walk) is also served by the Knaresborough-Wetherby bus.*

TERRAIN *Mostly good paths, some boggy sections.*

THE PUB

The Bay Horse is situated opposite the village cross and is a very attractive building dating back to 1600. The original beams are in evidence and it boasts an unusual circular, iron chandelier. The walls of the former barn are decorated with a Cat o'Nine Tails and a Ballmace. Over the open fireplace is a coat of arms of the Harewood family who previously owned the pub, and indeed the whole village. In 1958 the land, including the pub, was sold for £4200. The pub was once a staging post, and before that there was a Roman settlement in the area.

The Bay Horse has an Egon Ronay award for good food served at lunch and evening. Bar snacks and accommodation are available. There is also a beer garden. Opposite the pub is the former smithy, and a house dating back to Queen Anne's time.

Opening hours 12.00-2.30, 7.00-11.00

Draught beers Tetley Bitter; Whitbread Castle Eden Ale, Flowers IPA, Boddington Bitter

THE WALK

On leaving the pub turn left past the houses and turn left down Midgley Lane. Follow the signpost at the bottom to Plompton. This is a very good, clear, wide track leading to Goldsborough Mill Farm.

Cross the river Nidd and two main roads (with care, one is the A658) and follow the arrows on a good track past a caravan site leading to Birkham Wood. The river is on the right. follow the path on the edge of the wood, taking the left track at a fork to cross once again the A658.

Follow the arrows straight ahead and continue through the edge of the wood. At the end turn right to the end of the field, then turn left to follow a good track to Plompton Hall (see WALK 6). The route passes in front of this old and interesting building. Note the plaque *The Coach House 1760* on the wall.

Follow the metalled road to the left to Plompton High Grange. Pass round the farm to another hard, straight path through open fields to Loxley Farm. With the farm on the left, pass through Braham Wood out onto an open path and leading to Throstle Nest Farm.

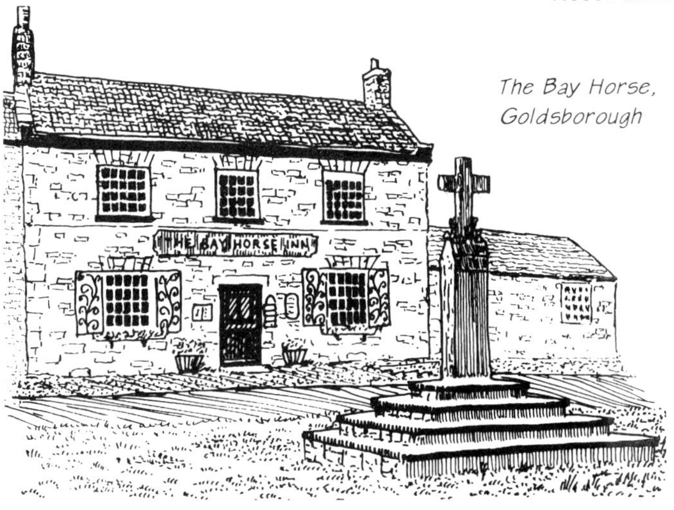

The Bay Horse, Goldsborough

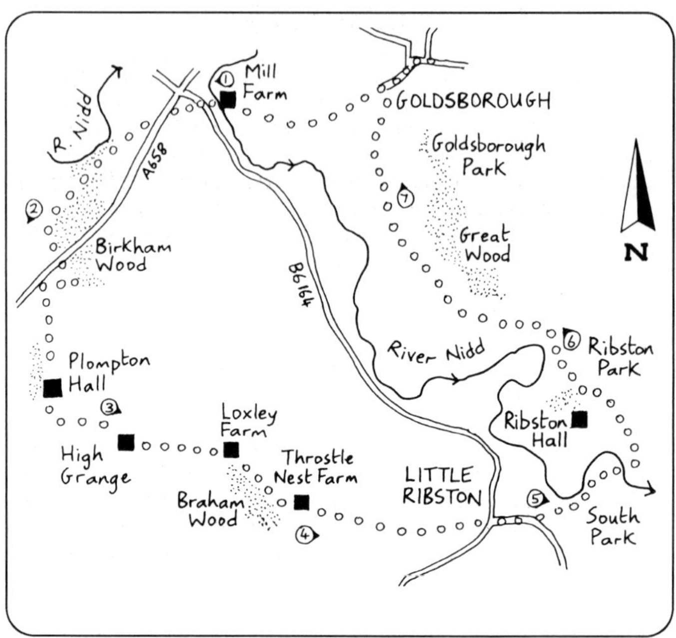

Turn right after the house and left at the end of the field to follow the hedge. Cross the middle of three fields, then right to reach a minor road. Turn left and then right on the main Knaresborough Road through Little Ribston.

After 200 yards, and where the road bends to the right, leave it on a good path leading to the river on the left. Continue on this metalled track to cross the imposing bridge. Veer left, passing Ribston Hall. *The long, red-brick Ribston Hall is the home of the Dent family. It was rebuilt for the Goodricke family in 1674, on the site of a 13th century building and chapel owned firstly by the Knights Templar, and later by the Knights of St John of Jerusalem, the Hospitallers.*

Pass into High Wood and out the other side bearing to the left to join a lane. This takes you back to Midgley Lane, and a right turn back to the Bay Horse.

GOLDSBOROUGH

Goldsborough is a pleasant community of houses in a quiet position, despite being so near a busy main road and only 2½ miles from Knaresborough. St Marys church boasts a Norman doorway, and much other early work, with a 14th century monument to a de Goldsborough knight. The church was the scene of a remarkable discovery in 1859, when a lead box was unearthed under the north wall during restoration work by Sir William Scott. It contained coins and silver. The coins had been minted in the ancient city of Bokhara in Russia. They were thought to have belonged to a trader who had dealings with merchants from the near east. The hoard was probably buried about the time of King Alfred in the 9th century, because it included a Saxon coin from his reign.

Richard de Goldsborough received the Manor House from William Rufus, the Conqueror's son. The family lived on the estate until the end of the 16th century, when after a family tussle, it went to Edwin Knightley, a relative by marriage. In retaliation, Richard Goldsborough later burned the place down.

Goldsborough's most important resident was the Princess Royal, daughter of King George V. She married Viscount Lascelles, before he became Lord Harewood. They moved into the hall in 1922 after their marriage, and lived there for seven years before moving to Harewood House. The red-brick hall dates from 1620, and hides from the outside world down the back lane leading to the church.

St Marys, Goldsborough

13

SPACEY HOUSES

START *Spacey Houses Inn, Spacey Houses Grid ref. 308514*

DISTANCE *6 miles*

MAP *Pathfinder 663 - Harrogate, and 672 - Harewood*

ACCESS *On the A658, 2 miles south of Harrogate. Served by Harrogate-Otley buses, and Harrogate-Leeds buses* ***and*** *trains*

TERRAIN *Easy, through rolling countyside.*

THE PUB

In days gone by, the Spacey Houses was a farmhouse owned by the Spacey family. In later days it was used as a coaching inn. Today it has been most attractively refurbished by Tetley's, whilst retaining its oak beams and original cast iron, moulded fireplaces. Emphasis is on fishing as a decorative feature on the walls, also old farm equipment and utensils.

It is a 'Big Steak House' offering an extensive menu, also a children's menu, Big Bites, luscious puddings and desserts. There are also Specials up on the board. There is food to cater for all tastes, and a beer garden.

In late January a special Burns' Night is hosted, with haggis and neeps and a Scottish Piper.

Opening hours
11.30-3.00, 5.30-11.00, and all day Friday and Saturday

Draught beers
Tetley Bitter

THE WALK

On leaving Spacey Houses, turn right and cross the road at the traffic lights. Turn right, and take the footpath on the left marked to Kirkby Overblow.

Take the stile at the end, turn right, then left through a gate. Cross the field diagonally to a gate, and once again cross diagonally to a gate in the right-hand corner. Continue with the hedge on the left straight on to the next stile, then turn left on to the main road.

Spacey Houses Inn

Go straight across the road through a gate, and cross the field to the corner and gate. Go around the field edge with a wall on the right. Cross the ditch by a lone hawthorn tree and up to a stile and the road.

Turn right, continue on the road beyond High Snape Farm and a bungalow on the left. Turn right at the footpath sign and gate. Continue across the field, aiming for two posts and then the hedge beyond. A footpath sign leads into Walton Head Lane.

Turn left down the lane for approximately a quarter of a mile, looking carefully for a concealed sign on the right. Go through the stile in the wall leading to a superior residence. The route crosses its driveway and into the church graveyard. Follow the path round the church to emerge at the Star and Garter at Kirkby Overblow (see WALK 9).

Continue down the road heading west out of the village, turning right past The Lodge and Birdwell Farm. At two houses on the left, take the signposted way opposite, on the right. Follow the track round the edge of the field with the fence on the right. Go through the next gate with the hedge now on the left. Through another gate at the top of the field, continue straight ahead with the hedge on the right and down to the beck.

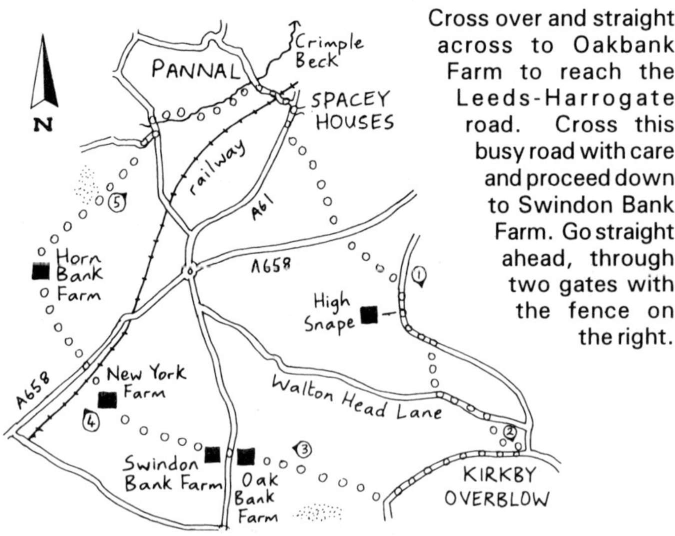

Cross over and straight across to Oakbank Farm to reach the Leeds-Harrogate road. Cross this busy road with care and proceed down to Swindon Bank Farm. Go straight ahead, through two gates with the fence on the right.

Go down the field to a gate and then straight down with the hedge on the right, to exit at a gate in the corner to cross the beck. Go straight ahead to cross another beck. Go through three more gates to the right of New York Farm to arrive at a level crossing leading to the road.

Cross the road to follow the track to Horn Bank Farm. At the farm turn right, then left with the farm on the left. Pass through the gate to the field-top. Turn right with the fence on the left. A viaduct is visible ahead, in the distance.

Head for the corner of the wood (The Warren) with the wall on the left. Go over the stile at the end of the wall. Head for the wood corner and Ringway sign, but do NOT follow it.

Continue with the wood on the left, leave the wood side to cross a field to a gate and stile. The hedge is now on the left, over a stile onto a fenced track to reach the road. Cross straight over to the next road. Straight across again to follow the Ringway footpath along the side of the Crimple Beck, a very picturesque section.

Follow the lane to the road, turn right passing the Pullman Dining Carriage at Platform One, Pannal railway station - time for afternoon tea?

PLATFORM ONE In the old railway station, this is an impressive conversion to licensed premises. One can sit out at the front and watch the trains go by. A great attraction here is the Pullman Dining Carriage, which is just what it says!

Pub opening hours 12.00-2.00, 7.00 (5.30 Fridays)-11.00

Draught beers Tetley Bitter; Burton Ale; guest beer

Head up to the main road and turn right back to the Spacey Houses Inn.

Pullman Dining Carriage, Platform One, Pannal

14

HAREWOOD

START *The Harewood Arms, Harewood Grid ref. 322452*

DISTANCE *6 miles*

MAP *Pathfinder 672 - Harewood*

ACCESS *On the A61, Harrogate to Leeds Road. Served by Leeds-Harrogate buses.*

TERRAIN *Easy, on good clear tracks*

THE PUB

The Harewood Arms offers very superior accommodation and dining facilities. There are 24 individually designed, en-suite bedrooms. A very comfortable bar serves morning coffee, lunches and afternoon teas. There is a superior restaurant for evening dinner: parties and conferences are catered for. The service is efficient and friendly and the food is as appealing to the palate as it is to the eye.

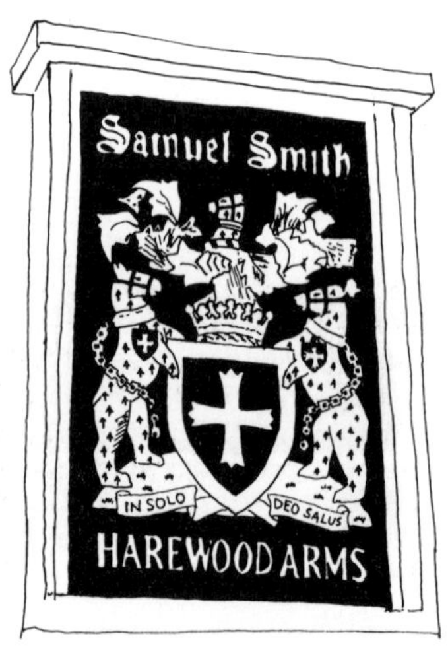

Opening hours

11.00-11.00

Draught beers

Samuel Smith
Old Brewery Bitter

THE WALK

The walk starts opposite the Harewood Arms and slightly to the right. Turn left on Church Lane. Follow the footpath sign to Stink along a leafy lane bordering the Harewood Estate (not at all smelly!). Note the gazebo hidden in the trees. On emerging from the trees there is a great view of rolling countryside, with Almscliff Crag on the skyline and the river Wharfe running in the valley below.

At a junction of paths, turn left over two cattle-grids on a good track between the buildings at Home Farm. Continue forward over the bridge and straight ahead up the hill. Follow the bridleway, passing through a gate with a wood on the right.

The Harewood Arms, Harewood

Turn right at a fork onto a narrow track with a wood on the right, leading to a barn and a small gate, now on the Ebor Way. This leads to a wood, turning right to follow the bridleway sign. At the next fork turn left up to the main junction of paths.

Take the Leeds Country Way on the left. Turn left to follow the bridleway through the wood. Turn left at the signpost on the Leeds Country Way. Turn right over the bridge through a gate, and the next gate following the fence on the left to emerge on the A61 Harrogate road.

Go straight across with care, following the signpost to Wike passing Lofthouse Farm. Turn left after 500 yards from the main road at a bridleway and blue arrow, still on the Leeds Country Way. Turn left at a signpost to Harewood, through a gate at the bottom. Here bear left with a wood on the right.

Turn right through a gate past Hollin Hall Pond and House. Pass to the right of the imposing house to two gates, and up to New Laithe Farm ahead, leading to the main road. Turn left on the road, then right through a field leading to a fence. Turn left on a good track leading back to the Harewood Arms.

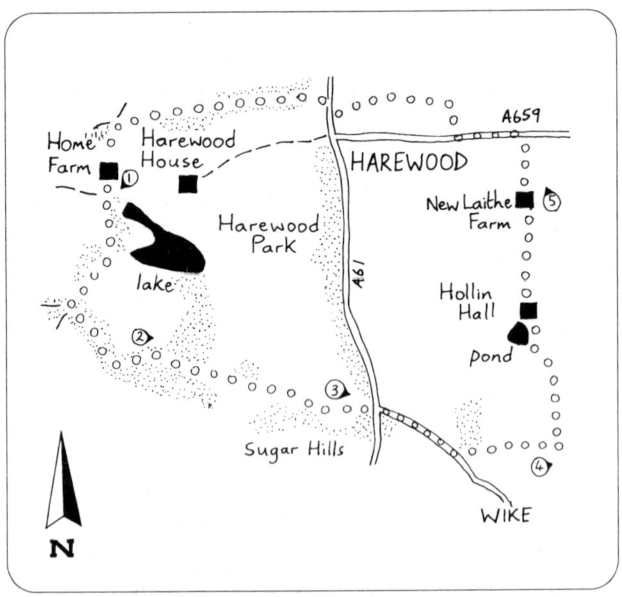

The Estate of Harewood is mentioned in the Domesday Book, and at the time of the Norman Conquest in 1066 belonged to Tor, Sprot and Grim, three Saxon chieftains. Early in the next century a castle was built against marauders from the North, and by 1209 Harewood was a prosperous market town. At one time there were no fewer than six public houses with twenty-two stage coaches passing through every day. The Harewood Arms is the only one remaining today, which dates back to 1815.

HAREWOOD HOUSE

It was Edwin Lascelles who commissioned John Carr of York and Robert Adam to build Harewood House and its model village in 1760, and in 1812 Edward Lascelles became the first Earl of Harewood. His rich source of income was from the sugar plantations of Barbados. The ownership has remained in the same family to this day.

The wife of the third Earl employed Sir Charles Barry to alter and enlarge the house in 1843 and to add the Terrace in the style of an Italian Palazzo. Today conditions of the stately manor have altered vastly, and now the house is open to the public. There are extensive grounds to walk in, and a bird garden to enjoy. It is well worth a visit.

In the grounds of the house is All Saints church. Though largely restored in 1863, it contains a number of medieval monuments, including one of Sir William Gascoigne, 1419. Hidden in trees to the north of the house are the remains of Harewood Castle.

Harewood House

ECCUP

START *The New Inn, Eccup* *Grid Ref. 289430*

DISTANCE *5½ miles*

MAP *Pathfinder 672 - Harewood*

ACCESS *On Otley Road, A659, past Arthington church, turn right up Rawdon Hill to Eccup. The A660 at Bramhope (mid-walk) is served by Leeds-Otley buses.*

TERRAIN *Easy, through fields and woods*

THE PUB

The New Inn is remotely situated but has a warm welcome for visitors with an open log fire. There is a restaurant, or bar snacks to suit all tastes. There is a large garden/play area at the rear, and also a family room.

Opening hours 11.30-3.00, 5.30-11.00

Draught beers Tetley Bitter
Marston Pedigree

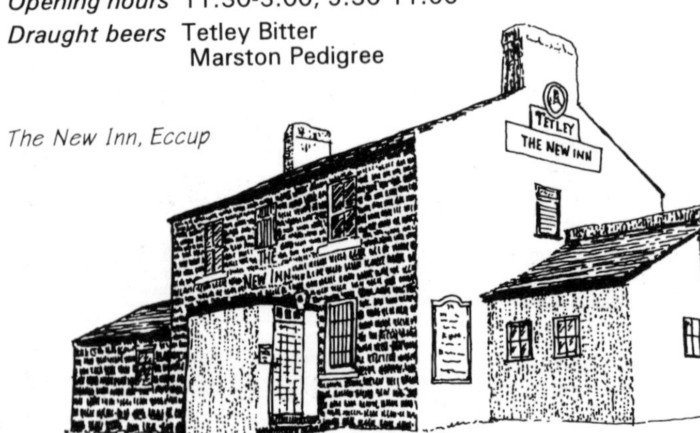

The New Inn, Eccup

THE WALK

On leaving the pub turn left along the road to the first signpost. Here turn right over two stiles and ahead to a gate. Follow the track to a tree with arrows. Here go diagonally right to a stile in the wall near the wood. Cross the field towards the building at Lineham Farm, and follow the path on the side of it and over the stile ahead. Follow the fence on the left which becomes a wall leading towards a farm and the road. Turn left on the road and quickly right to Breary Cottage.

Cross over a stile by a gate and between the farm buildings. Proceed down the field and over a stile and the next fields with stiles to the main road. Cross by the garage and down the Sycamores. Turn left after the rugby field, down the field with a ditch and fence on the left to cross over a stile at the bottom. Continue forward with a wood on the right. At the next stile and a gate, turn left towards a barn to arrive at a gate into a wood.

Go straight ahead, turning right up to Fish Pond. Walk along the edge of the pond and over a wooden bridge and through the gate ahead. Head up the line of trees to a lane. Turn left to Cocker Hill Farm. Pass through the farm buildings and down the lane to the main road. Cross over and turn right past the Parkway Hotel. Time for afternoon tea? You will need to take your boots off!

Turn left down the side of the hotel. Turning left over a stile and right over a bridge, now in Golden Acre Park with the lake on the left. Turn right through a small gate and left onto the Meanwood Valley Trail. Head up this enclosed way to the road. Straight across, turn right up King Lane passing Clonmore Farm entrance. Turn left into the wood to follow the fence on the left to the end of the wood. At the lane turn right to a junction, then left back to the New Inn.

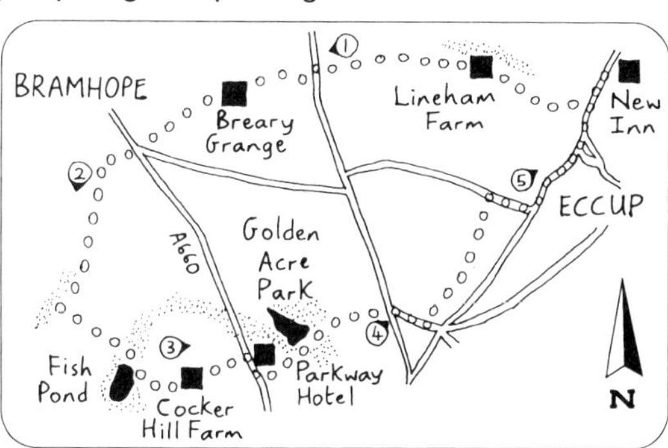

16

LINTON

START *The Windmill Inn, Linton* *Grid ref. 392468*

DISTANCE *8½ miles*

MAP *Pathfinder 663 - Harrogate, and 672 - Harewood*

ACCESS *Off the Harewood-Wetherby road (A659) at Collingham. Served by the Leeds-Wetherby bus. Kirk Deighton (mid-walk) is served by the Wetherby-Knaresborough bus.*

TERRAIN *Easy, good lanes.*

THE PUB

The Windmill is a truly old-world country pub. It is very old, dating back to 1314 when it was a residence of the owner of the nearby windmill. In 1674 it became a coaching inn and has been a pub ever since. There is a secret passage connected to the church, no doubt used in times of persecution of the clergy. The old character still remains in its oak beams, stone walls, open fireplaces and rooms on different levels.

The food is varied and substantial. Parties of up to 50 are catered for. Special Bonfire Night and Christmas Eve fancy dress evenings are held. There is a beer garden at the rear.

Opening hours
11.30-3.00, 5.30-11.00

Draught beers
Theakston Bitter, XB; Younger Scotch, No.3

THE WALK

The walk starts opposite the pub on the route to Woodhall along Trip Lane. At the end turn right on the footpath to Sicklinghall (Ebor Way), passing through Lime Kiln Wood into a field. Go along the edge of the field to turn right round the outside of the wood, to then enter the wood. Turn right along the edge to enter a field to emerge onto a lane by Sicklinghall House.

Turn right along Longlands Lane to emerge on the road through Sicklinghall (see WALK 18). Turn right past the pond, and then left down Stockeld Lane. Sicklinghall Lodge and a nursery are passed to enter a wood, and next the parkland of Stockeld Park House. This dates in part from the mid-18th century.

The Windmill, Linton

Keep on the main track to cross the main road (A661) to Stockeld Grange. Cross over a cattle-grid to the left of the farm. Go straight ahead through a gate to another gate and a road.

Go straight across to a field track, across a bridge and round the field edge, passing through the hedge to the other side. Kirk Deighton church is ahead. Restored in 1875, All Saints church possesses a Norman doorway, and a tall spire resting on a solid tower base. The lane emerges at the Bay Horse.

THE BAY HORSE, Kirk Deighton. At one time in the distant past two pubs used to stand here, side by side, 'The Black Horse' and 'The Greyhound'. In 1927 the Black Horse became the Bay Horse. Outside you will find horse tethers. There was a knacker yard nearby and after selling the poor horse, the money was spent in the pub!

A good variety of sandwiches and hot and cold food, though none on Sundays.

Opening hours 12.00-2.30 (Sat 3.00), 6.00-11.00

Draught beers John Smith Bitter; Stones Bitter

The Bay Horse, Kirk Deighton

Turn right past the pub and right down the cul-de-sac and enclosed lane. At a junction turn left along the field edge to turn left again through the hedge to emerge onto a track. Go straight across, bearing left on the field edge to reach the A661 again.

Turn left on the road towards Wetherby. At the road junction turn right past the former hospital. Turn left down to the river past the John Bradley plaque, down the steps, through the gate, and turn right.

Through the field onto the golf course practice field, turn right and along the side of a field to turn under a railway arch. Follow a broad green track across the golf course (with care), up to the road. Turn left, passing all the fantastic properties to Linton.

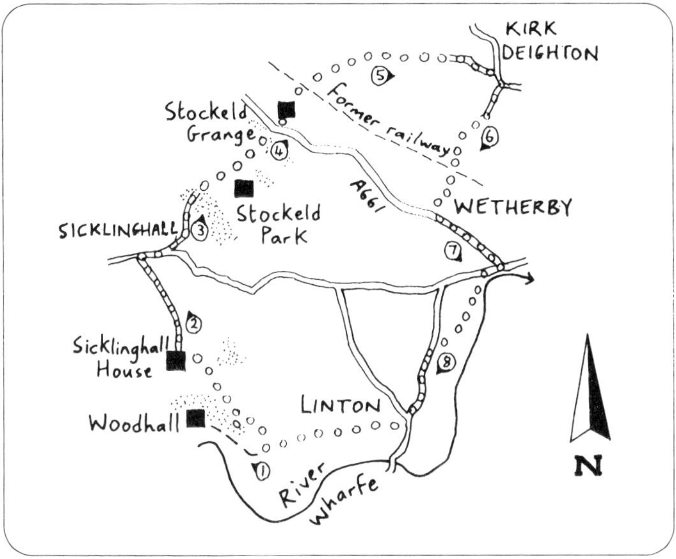
KIRK
DEIGHTON
5
Former railway
Stockeld
Grange
4
6
A661
WETHERBY
Stockeld
Park
SICKLINGHALL
3
7
2
Sicklinghall
House
8
LINTON
Woodhall
1
River
Wharfe
N

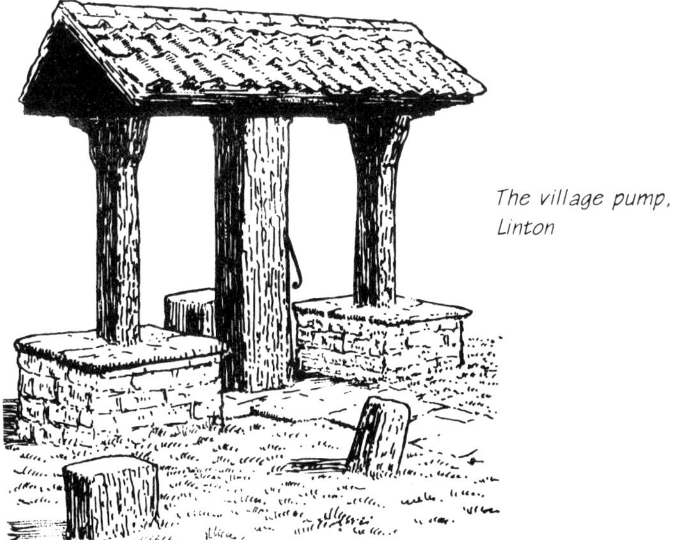

The village pump, Linton

17

ARTHINGTON

START *The Wharfedale, Arthington Grid ref. 260450*

DISTANCE *8½ miles*

MAP *Pathfinder 672 - Harewood*

ACCESS *On the A659 between Pool Bridge and Harewood. Leeds-Otley and Otley-Harrogate buses run through Pool.*

TERRAIN *Easy field paths, partly on the Dales Way link and the Ebor Way*

THE PUB

The Wharfedale is a country pub and restaurant with that extra touch, its genial Italian host - Tino. You can be assured of good food in a friendly atmosphere. Bar food is served seven days per week: the restaurant is open Tuesday to Saturday evenings.

There is dancing every Friday and Saturday after dinner until midnight. There is also a beer garden. The inn holds a 'Choice' award recognised by Leeds City Council Environmental Health Department for excellent standards of hygiene. What more could you want?

Alongside, the Leeds-Harrogate railway is carried high above the road.

Opening hours
11.30-3.00, 6.30-11.00

Draught beers
Tetley Bitter

THE WALK

After a good lunch we drove further up the road to park at Arthington church. St Peters, with its tall spire, dates from 1864. One mile further east along the main road is the Nunnery, a beautiful, 3-storeyed building of 1585.

Take the footpath at the right-hand side of the church marked to Eccup. Turn left at the top of the field behind the church. Pass through the gate at the end and turn right. Pass through two more gates then diagonally left towards the woods.

Enter Blanket Wood by a stile. Bear right up the field to a post with a yellow mark. Proceed up the field towards Bank Side Farm and up to the stile and sign-post to Eccup on Bank Top Lane. Bear left to the stile in the fence, and up the field with the fence on the left to the next stile.

The Wharfedale, Arthington

Continue to the top of the field, turn left over a stile, the fence now on the right. After another stile, take the stile on the right by a gate. Continue on the grassy track to a gate and stile, take the next stile in the wall on the left to cross a short field to the road.

Turn left, and immediately on the right is the footpath sign. Cross the centre of a large field towards a telegraph pole and then a wall-stile leading to another stile onto a track. Turn right, leading to the road.

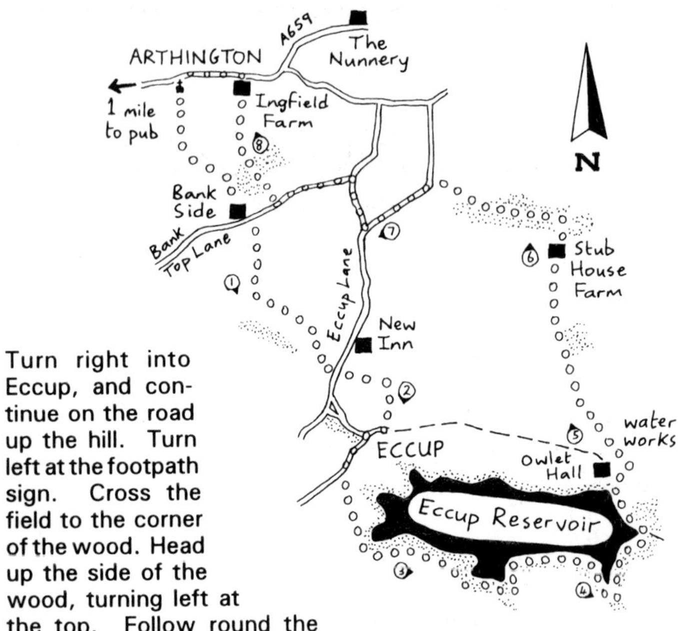

Turn right into Eccup, and continue on the road up the hill. Turn left at the footpath sign. Cross the field to the corner of the wood. Head up the side of the wood, turning left at the top. Follow round the outside of the wood to a small white gate leading to an enclosed way and a road.

Turn left, passing the waterworks house and enter Eccup Reservoir grounds through a white gate. Follow the reservoir track right round. Leave the reservoir at the end of the embankment. Continue straight forward and then round to the right. Take a footpath sign on the left to come back to the road.

Turn left, then quickly right on a bridlepath through a gate. Continue in the same direction, passing through two more gates to arrive at a gate on the left. Continue, passing Stub House Farm. At the bottom, turn left onto the Ebor Way, through the wood to reach the road.

Turn left up the hill. Turn right down Bedlam Lane, then turn left on the bridleway of Allums Lane. Before the gate to Bank Side Farm turn right down the enclosed track leading to Ingfield Farm and the main road. Turn left back to Arthington church.

18

SICKLINGHALL

START *The Scotts Arms, Sicklinghall Grid ref. 360485*

DISTANCE *6½ miles*

MAP *Pathfinder 663 - Harrogate, 672 - Harewood*

ACCESS *2½ miles west of Wetherby. Served by Wetherby-Harrogate schoolday bus. Spofforth (just off-route) is on the main Harrogate-Wetherby bus route.*

TERRAIN *Fields and tracks, could be muddy.*

THE PUB

The Scotts Arms was a mass of flowers on my visit, most attractive. It was just as interesting inside with its atmosphere and good food. In addition to bar meals there is also a restaurant with a gourmet menu or an excellent a la carte menu.

Families are welcome, and there is a very good garden and play area.

Opening hours

12.00-3.00, 6.00-11.00

Draught beers

Younger Scotch, No.3
Theakston Bitter, Old Peculier

In the grounds of the Catholic church, Sicklinghall

THE WALK

Start from the back of the car park, through a stile and round the stables to a stile in the corner. Continue straight ahead over two stiles. Turn left, round the field to a stile on the left. Turn right to a gate, and then right on a broad track to Whin Lane Farm.

Enter the farmyard and turn to follow a broad track to the corner of a wood. Continue on the track heading for Spofforth to reach High Lane. Turn left to a junction, here turn right into Low Lane to reach a farm. Continue on the track to reach the driveway to Park House Farm.

Scotts Arms, Sicklinghall

Turn up the driveway and in front of the farm leading to a fenced, grass track to a gate into a field. Continue straight ahead to cross the beck at a rusty iron gate and up to Parks Farm. Keep to the left of the buildings and round through the gate onto a track. Turn right into the farmyard and pass in front of the very attractive farmhouse to a yellow arrow at a gate.

Cross the field to a stile in the corner of the fence. Walk down with the fence on the left to a stile. Bear right to a stile in the corner and cross two streams. Turn right and through a gate towards Low Hall. Go through a gate into the farmyard on a 'preferred way', through a gate and up the side of a wall onto the road at All Saints primary school, Kirkby Overblow.

Kirkby Overblow was mentioned in the Domesday Book. It took its name from the ore blowers when the area was rich in iron deposits in the Middle Ages. In 1302 its name was recorded as Kirkby Orblowers. The village once had a moated hall which was burnt by the Royalists during the Civil War. All Saints church is a lovely building in the heart of the village.

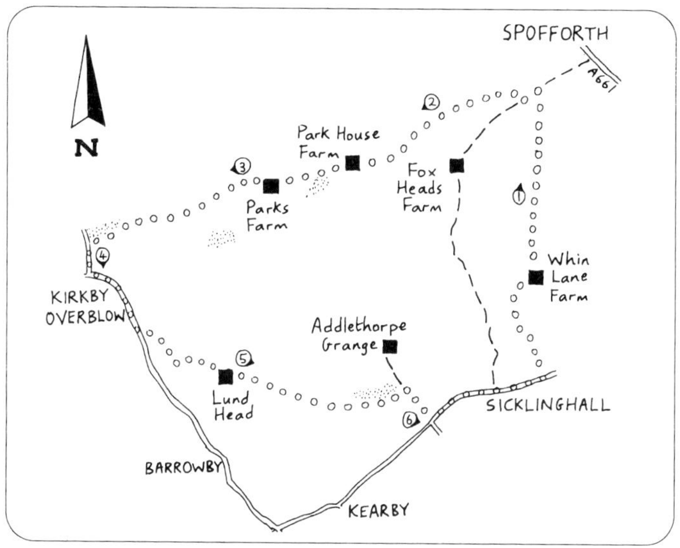

Turn left on the road to the Shoulder of Mutton, (see WALK 9). Turn left again along the road to Barrowby. Continue past the houses and turn left onto the track of Marsh Lane at the footpath sign. Pass Lund Head Farm and continue down the enclosed track into the open field. Go straight ahead, with the fence on the left. Follow the narrow track to a small gate to eventually reach a lane.

Go straight across to a gate with a fence on the right. Continue ahead to a small wooden gate. Cross the field to reach a farm track, turn right. At the next track (Addlethorpe Grange drive) turn right again, leading to the road to Sicklinghall. Turn left to return to the Scotts Arms.

19

NORTH RIGTON

START *The Square and Compass, North Rigton*
Grid ref. 281493

DISTANCE *5½ miles*

MAP *Pathfinder 672 - Harewood*

ACCESS *Off the A658 Otley to Harrogate Road, along which buses run. Weeton (mid-walk) has a station on the Leeds-Harrogate line.*

TERRAIN *Easy field paths, with interesting views from Almscliff Crag.*

THE PUB

The Square and Compass is an up-market venue for lunch, offering a very different choice of sandwiches. The new, cosy brasserie-style restaurant serves traditional English dishes with more than a hint of Yorkshire, the emphasis being on quality, freshness and value for money. Weekend brunch can start with Bucks Fizz, scrambled eggs with smoked salmon, eggs benedict or a full Yorkshire breakfast.

Opening hours
11.30-2.00, 6.30-11.00

Draught beers
Younger Scotch, No.3

The stocks, North Rigton

THE WALK

On leaving the hotel turn right round the side of the building and up the hill. After the last house on the right (Highfold), take the footpath on the left to Almscliff Crag. Follow the arrow into the overgrown paddock and over the stile on the left. Turn right into the enclosed way leading to the road.

Turn right on the road, and past New House Farm turn right over a stile. Continue diagonally left through the field to another stile and straight across the access road, in the same direction: a wall is now on the right. Almscliff Crag is now in view. Continue heading for it, and up the steep incline. *Almscliff Crag is a major landmark in the Wharfe Valley, prominent in views from all over the district. Perched amongst neatly packaged green fields, it is a hugely popular venue for climbers who test their skills on the rough gritstone.* Pass through the stile in between the rocks and down. Turn left at the bottom and follow the fence around to a stile leading to a road. Turn left on the road.

The Square & Compass, North Rigton

At Cliff House turn right through a white gate and over a stile into a field. Go diagonally across to a stile, then left down the side of the field to a stile in the corner. Go down through a gate leading to a flagged way to Holly Hill Farm.

At the cattle-grid turn right without crossing it, along the back of the farm and through a gate. The hedge is now on the right, leading to a stile at the bottom. Cross over the stream, over a stile and into a field. A fence is now on the left, to reach a stile by a gate and down to a road.

Go straight across the road into a narrow, enclosed path. Turn left at the bottom, over a stile into a field to emerge onto the road at Huby. Turn right on the road passing Weeton station.

After 300 yards on the road take a hidden stile on the left by trees. Continue up the field to a gate and forward onto another road. Turn left on the road passing Manor Farm. There is a walk of approximately a mile on this country road. Weeton church is in view ahead.

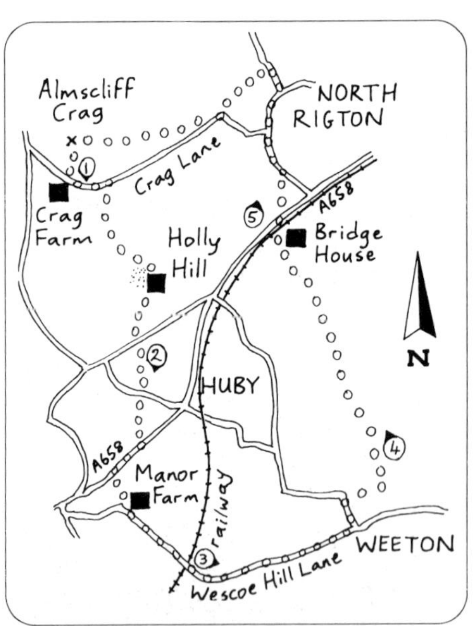

Past Wescoe House, turn left at the road junction to Huby. At the bend in the road turn right into a hedged way leading to a lane.

Turn left down the lane to its end, over a stile and straight ahead to cross a tiny bridge to a stile in the fence. Cross the field to a tree, and up the side of a fence to a gate. Through the gate turn left, then over a stile into a drive, and up it.

Cross over the railway bridge onto the road. Turn right and quickly left through a small gate before the Square and Compass sign on the main road. Head diagonally across the field to a white gate in the corner and onto the road at the imposing residence of Rigton Chase House. Turn up the road back to North Rigton and the Square and Compass.

20

POOL IN WHARFEDALE

START *The White Hart, Pool Grid ref. 245451*

DISTANCE *6½ or 8½ miles*

MAP *Pathfinder 672 - Harewood*

ACCESS *At the junction of A659 and A658. Served by Otley-Leeds and Otley-Harrogate buses.*

TERRAIN *Varied fields, quiet roads, wood and riverside*

THE PUB

The White Hart has an old world atmosphere with its beams and oak tables. The food is very good - ample portions of tasty, attractively served food. In summer one can dine outside, and there is a children's play area and also a family room. The front was a mass of flowers and looked most appealing on my visit.

Opening hours 11.00-11.00

Draught beers Taylor Landlord; Stones Bitter; Worthington Best Bitter; guest beer

The White Hart, Pool

THE WALK

Turn right on leaving the White Hart and walk to Pool Bridge. Cross the Wharfe and take a stile on the left. Walk diagonally across the field to the road. Cross over and slightly left to the footpath sign. Walk up the side of the hedge to a stile in the top corner, follow the hedge round and up the field to the sheep pen. Follow the yellow arrow up the field with a fence on the right.

Pass over two stiles leading to Hilltop Farm. Walk through the farmyard to the road. Turn right up the road, over the bridge and up the other side to the road junction at Stainburn.

FOR THE LONGER WALK continue up the hill past St. Marys church. Beyond it, the next feature of interest is the attractive hamlet of Braythorn. At the top of the hill turn right, with Almscliff Crag ahead.

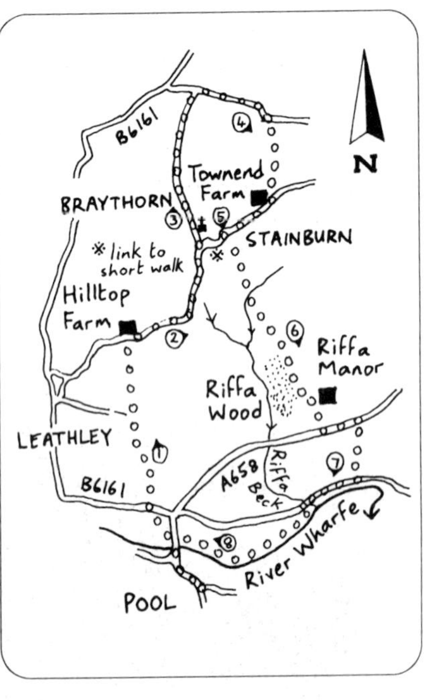

When the road turns left, take the green bridleway straight ahead to reach a metal gate, and through a field to the next gate. Continue down the field to a small wooden gate leading to the road.

Turn right past Townend Farm and a Stainburn sign, down the hill to the bridleway sign on the left at a metal gate.

FOR THE SHORTER WALK turn right at the junction to the bridleway on the right.

FOR BOTH WALKS continue through the gate to reach another, and down a good track leading to a gate and enclosed way. Continue in the same direction, through metal gates, over a bridge and up to a gate-post and wooden gate ahead, the fence now on the left.

Continue forward, ignoring a gate on the left with a blue arrow, to reach a gate ahead. Cross field and stile with Riffa Wood on the right. Turn right into the wood at a small gate with arrows. Turn left along the top of the wood. Fight your way through the undergrowth to a gate and the road.

Pass down Riffa Manor driveway to the main road, and turn left. After 450 yards, take the footpath on the right leading down to the river Wharfe. Turn right to follow the river back to Pool Bridge and then go left, back to the White Hart.

Now standing redundant, parts of this tiny church date back to Norman times.

St Marys, Stainburn

INDEX

Villages and principal features: pubs in italics (walk number refers)